WHAT PEOPLE ARE SAYING
ABOUT GINA

Gina Radke is a force for the aviation industry, entrepreneurship, and the success of women in industry and leadership.
—Dr. Teri Cox, *Cox Consulting*

I've had the opportunity to experience Gina's extraordinary leadership.
—Dr Adam Arroyos, *Grandslam Performance Associates*

Gina Radke is driven to be the best wife, mother, leader, businessowner, motivator, and role model.
—Rickey McCauley, *Retired Chief Information Officer*

Gina is a proven, dynamic leader who uses her influence to empower and encourage others.
—Lori Burrows, *Chief Legal Counsel, Electric Utilities Company*

Gina is a visionary leader who transforms whatever she touches.
—Chris Dendy, *Proposal Manager, Hewlet Packard*

Gina is an exceptional business and thought leader.
—Jacob Addie, *Director of Human Resources, J. B. Hunt Transportation*

T0151733

WHAT PEOPLE ARE SAYING
ABOUT *MORE THAN*

Be inspired! Change your thinking, in fact expand your thinking. Inspiring read!

—Tony Jeary, *The RESULTS Guy*™

Gina's specific examples of how she has persevered as a female business leader really hit home. We all have experienced versions of her stories. Her advice is smart and refreshing, and really lays out particular tactics to overcome, work hard, and most importantly, build the life you want to build.

—Lisa Song Sutton, *Investor, Founder Sin City Cupcakes, Former Miss Nevada*

Gina is a game changer! Her experiences as a leader and trail blazer are invaluable. This is a book every entrepreneur and executive needs.

—Tammy Kling, *CEO OnFire Books Leadership Company*

This writing of the book is enjoyable and thrilling all the way, with many personal experiences and a great deal of inspiration. One of the biggest strengths of the book is the extensive coverage on male allies. I think it is a great way to bandwagon some of leading men working on gender equity quotient.

—Rupa Dash, *Founder World Women Summit, Dash Global Media*

more than

HOW TO BE BOLD
AND BALANCED IN
LIFE AND BUSINESS

GINA RADKE

Clovercroft Publishing

More Than

Published by Clovercroft Publishing, Franklin, Tennessee

Edited by Christy Callahan

Cover Design by Nelly Sanchez

Interior Design by Suzanne Lawing

Printed in the United States of America

978-1-950892-04-4

Dedication
To my loving ally and husband, Wade.
You put me in the ring.

*To the Strong Women who raised me. I will continue
the tradition of changing the world!*

Contents

ACKNOWLEDGMENTS

So many great women have helped to lift me up, starting with my family—my grandmother, Helen Webb, my mother, Sharon McGlothin, and my stepmother, Elizabeth Hayward. Then there was one of my high school teachers, Mrs. Cindy Holmes, who taught me about humility, which I now define as power and confidence under control. I certainly wouldn't be where I am today without my tribe of executive women: Dr. Tionna Jenkins, Elizabeth Solano, Lori Burrows, and Dr. Teri Cox, each of whom contributes to the male-dominated industries in which they work. And I can't forget one of my dearest friends and mentors, Brandi Schroeder, who I have known longer than just about anyone. Katherine Daniels is a woman I met when she was working at a business magazine that I had been featured in. Katherine quickly become a mentor to me in world of building your brand. She is very knowledgeable about building a brand and was happy to share her wisdom with me. All of these women have helped to heal my soul and empowered me when I was down at various times in my life. And that's just naming a few. I didn't do it alone, and all the help I received along the way has inspired me to speak life into the women I meet.

INTRODUCTION

Have you ever been judged based on your sex? It's a cliché, but working as a woman in a man's field, I deal with gender bias on a daily basis. I own Galley Support Innovations, an aerospace design and manufacturing company in Arkansas. My company is responsible for the locks and latches you see when entering a commercial aircraft (most famously, the Occupied/Vacant latch on the airplane's bathroom door). When the company was started, we had a total of $10,459 sales for the year. After 14 years of hard work, sacrifice, and blood, sweat, and tears, we are now a multimillion dollar company with customers in over 13 different countries. Coincidentally, the co-owner of my business is my husband of more than twenty years, Wade, whom I love with all my heart. But no matter the love, I often believe that owning the company with him actually makes it harder for me to be a woman in manufacturing. Once people hear that we own the company together, I can almost read their thoughts: *Oh, she doesn't really work there.* And I'm sure they wouldn't be thinking that if we owned a bridal shop or the like.

That's followed by comments like, "Are you the owner for tax purposes?" Or my favorite: "Do you do your husband's books?" (Now add "little lady" with a knowing smile.) Next come the jokes aimed at my husband: "So, you work under her?" Hilarious, I know. If I don't tell people that Wade and I work together, I'll often get the question, "How did you get into this business?"

Once I explain that we started the company together and that the product line was a family business started by his grandfather, they seem more at ease, likely because they can still give credit to my husband. Yes, the business did originally belong to my husband's family, but Wade didn't know his father or anyone on his father's side of the family until he was 30, just one year before we started our own company and purchased the family company's product line. In other words, Wade didn't grow up in the company, and it wasn't handed down to him. We took the company, and together we turned it into what it is today.

I get why women often feel the need to explain why they own a business in a male-dominated field, or even explain why they chose to work in one. It's because rarely do people seem satisfied by the explanation, "I like what I do, and I saw an opportunity to make money doing it."

Things are changing, though, albeit slowly. The United States government's Small Business Administration has a Woman Owned Small Business (WOSB) Program with the goal of providing a percentage of government contracts to businesses that are at least 51 percent owned and operated by women. Even with the goal of federal contracts being awarded to women-owned businesses at a minuscule 5 percent, that goal has only been met once (2015) since the inception of the program in 1994. It took 21 years for the feds to meet that goal the first time, and more than 95 percent of contract awards still go to male-owned businesses.[1]

The program is needed for business diversity, and it's a great idea, but the true measure of the program—having more female-owned businesses earning government contract work—is eclipsed by those men who don't follow the rules and either claim a woman as the owner of the business or put the business in a woman's name to earn more contracts. Since that has become so common, many people just assume that it's the case with my business, and that only gives them another reason to discount me as a legitimate CEO.

Once, at a Small Business Administration reception, Wade and I were chatting with another couple. Like me, the woman was in manufacturing and owned her own business. As we talked, we were approached by a contract specialist with a government agency who said, "Let me guess. Women-owned businesses?" He then proceeded to turn his back to the women and speak to our husbands about doing business with the agency he represented because he assumed that the two men he was speaking with were the real owners and that their wives simply held the title. Basically, he assumed that as couples who owned businesses together, we were engaged in a ruse to beat the system, and apparently he couldn't begin imagine that "the little ladies"

---

1 For statistics on women in leadership, see Judith Warner, "Women's Leadership by the Numbers," Center for American Progress, March 7, 2014, https://www.americanprogress.org/issues/women/reports/2014/03/07/85457/ fact-sheet-the-womens-leadership-gap/.

might be the real decision-makers.

The contract specialist didn't get too far before Wade quickly shut him down. "I just design parts," he said. "My wife really does run the business. If you want to talk about contracts, you'll have to speak to her."

The other woman's husband explained that he was in the military and had nothing to do with her business. In other words, the husbands had to explain to the male contract specialist that their wives were legitimate business owners.

Now, to my husband's credit, he does much more than just design parts. And even more to his credit, he knows how much I've had to overcome as a woman in my field, so he is an ally who makes sure my work is recognized. However, I never wanted my gender to define me or my career path. What's funny is, just as the gullies and slopes to large degree determine how and where water flows downhill, my being a woman has definitely defined my road to achievement different from what it would have been were I a male.

When I decided to write a book, I wanted to write a generic business book about the lessons I learned along the way, devoid of any gender references. I didn't want to sell books just because I am a woman in a man's field. I wanted to be seen for my intellect, business acumen, and accomplishments, not for my lack of a penis. However, the more I wrote, the more I noticed that women encounter obstacles that are very different from our male counterparts, even though many steps leading to success are similar.

There are literally hundreds of books on business leadership and motivation written by men, but a smaller percentage of books on business success are written by women. So, I had to face the facts. Maybe it was the fact that I was born with ovaries that overly qualifies me to write this book since those ovaries are responsible for many of the experiences I have gained over the years.

I am motivated by all the women who have come to me and asked that I be their mentor. I want to fill the void for hardworking women who are looking for answers and assurances that they are not alone—women who are looking for someone who experienced the struggles they are currently facing and came out on top. I want to empower women and help them find their voice.

> I want to empower women and help them find their voice.

I want to contribute to the conversation that was started by so many great women before me. We need to look out for each other. The world today has enough division. I want this book to reach across the divide to transcend status, age, race, and any other barrier we place between those we perceive as being different. I want this book to empower women and help them realize they are not alone. I want this book to help women see that others not only have the same struggles and hardships, but that they can overcome those struggles and hardships as well.

Like anything in life, we view the world through the lens of our own personal experiences, so I couldn't help but write a book for women about something that I have years of experience with. Even though being a woman in a primarily male field has shaped my point of view, this book is for all women, no matter your place in business or your career. It's for the salon owner who holds her ground and negotiates solid contracts with her vendors. It's for the woman in sales who works late hours and still manages to return home in time to give the kids a bath. It's for the female entrepreneur who has a hard time getting financing because she doesn't have a male CEO. This book is for any woman who tries to have both a successful career and a well-balanced life. It doesn't matter if that includes a significant other and 2.5 kids or living a fabulous life without a romantic partner. And it doesn't matter if that life consists of a career as a stay-at-home mom raising the next generation of world changers; there will be sections of this book that will make you want to scream, "Yes! Me too!"

> Gender is not the final word on defining us any more than it enables us.

Being a woman is who we are, but our gender is not the final word on defining us any more than it enables us. None of us—humans all—can be defined by a single trait. We are a combination of who we love, who we serve, who we raise, and finally what we do for a living. We are who we are in public, who we are in private, and who we are when surrounded by those closest to us. We are the sum of our past, good or bad, the moment of our present, and the hopes of our future. We cannot be confined or defined by a single word or a catchphrase. We are glorious, gritty, tender, and tough. We are beautiful, intelligent, talented, creative, and hardworking. It's time we take everything we are and learn to make it work for us. Yes, there are still mountains to climb and stereotypes to overcome, but we can do it and we *are* doing it!

CHAPTER 1

MORE THAN JUST A BUSINESS BITCH

Last year, I was in the middle of a six-million-dollar contract negotiation with a customer's male representative. He was trying to pressure me into giving up more than a hundred thousand dollars in product for the customer's marketing use with no assurance that my company could use the product photos for our marketing materials. I couldn't believe what I was hearing. *Is this how other companies do business?* Why would anyone in their right mind pay a hundred thousand dollars for a marketing campaign that they didn't have the rights to use?

It was a lopsided deal that had no upside for my company. There was no way I was going to agree to sell my business short by giving him what he wanted. I pushed back and tried to negotiate a fair arrangement. Like any business owner, when I negotiate contracts I work hard to ensure that I get the best possible outcome for my employees, my business, and my customers. Often, that means taking hard lines on terms that would potentially damage my business. It also means not contracting with suppliers that do not treat my company like the sophisticated business that it is. I also won't tolerate a supplier that is going to treat me like I am ignorant of what they're trying to get away with just because I'm a female.

I had been in negotiation, exchanging emails with the man for a while, but one morning I received an email—clearly sent to me by accident—that read, "She's going to give it to us eventually, but she's being a bitch about the marketing chapter."

I was stunned! Seeing that word literally knocked me back in my chair and landed like a slap to the face. I couldn't decide if I wanted to cry or throw my laptop against the wall. How dare this man sink so low as to call me a bitch in a business email! I felt violated. I mistakenly assumed I was working with a professional, not an emotional man who would throw that word around when he didn't get his way.

Obviously, I wasn't supposed to see that email. He must have accidentally hit Reply All instead of forwarding the document to the intended recipient. He was implying that since I wouldn't give him what he wanted that I was being a "bitch."

While I was furious, I did not take immediate action, and I got the last laugh in the end. Thanks to his lovely email, I was able to get what I needed for marketing without having to report him or go to his boss. Instead, within two hours of his "bitch" email, I received another email informing me that the other company would agree to share the product marketing images with my company. I ended up doing business with them. Surprised? Why did I allow my company to enter into contract with them? Because I got the deal we needed for my company to make a profit. It was irrelevant that I was personally attacked—what mattered is that it was a great deal for my company.

In the end, we got the right result, but it should have happened without the offensive message and without me having to be treated as less than just because I was a woman who had the nerve to stand up for my company's interests. It's unacceptable to the integrity of any business to accept that kid of behavior, and reading that word used in reference to me and my business actions in an email did sting. It was an unexpected, undeserved, and mean-spirited slap across the face as I sat in what I thought was my safe place— my office. The office for which I pay the bills to keep the lights on and own as the CEO. The same office that pushes forward the company I spent countless hours working to build. The office that I've been using to help create a safe place for women. Oh yeah, it stung, but it didn't break me. And I look back on it now and see how it made me better. In fairness, God only knows what he would've called me if I were a man—no way I'm the only person he's been rude about behind their back. Part of success is being the better person and responding the way your mentors have modeled and exhorted you to respond. I think of it as leadership—if everyone were nice and fair, it would be easier, but nobody needs a good example when everything is fair and rosy.

Trust me, that's not that the only time that I've heard the "Big Bad B-Word" thrown my way, or in the direction of another woman trying to stand up for herself or her business. I've heard it countless times during my career. Once, I was on a professional association board for my industry that had to make some difficult budget decisions. I disagreed with the loudest male member of the group and spoke my mind about where I thought the money should go. Shortly after, I learned that he loudly referred to me as the "uppity bitch" of the group while exiting the meeting.

Bitch is an easy word for both men and women to use when they aren't happy with a woman. I personally have been called a "bulldog," "the toughest thing in a skirt," and, of course, a "bitch."

I'm not a "fair, but stern" professional. I'm a bitch.

I'm not a "good business person." I'm a bitch.

An aggressive man is often thought of as a go-getter, but an aggressive woman gets labeled as a bitch. What's funny is that I've heard plenty of men get called an asshole only for that to be followed by, "Yeah, but he's good at what he does." Being good at what he does is what defines him professionally, not the fact that he's a complete jerk who degrades others to get ahead. Men are allowed to be both good businessmen and assholes at the same time.

On the other hand, women who act aggressively on behalf of their business interests, regardless of how they conduct themselves as individuals, are called bitches. That label is often what defines a strong woman in business, no matter how nice she is to be around or how she treats the other people she associates with professionally. Rarely will a woman be viewed as being nice and having good business sense.

Despite the reputation I have for standing up and fighting for what I think is right for my business, I am much more than just "a business bitch." That's why I wanted to initially title this book *More than Just a Business Bitch*. I know that *bitch* is an emotionally charged word that would definitely get attention sitting on a bookshelf or as you scroll through your online library of choice. It was also an unintentional nod to Kelly Kapoor on *The Office,* who coined the phrase "business bitch." My love for Mindy Kaling and the characters she has portrayed has apparently had an influence on my daily life.

Many women use the word as a term of endearment, as in, "What's up, bitches?" Does that sound familiar? How many of you have said things like, "I'm not trying to be a bitch, but I don't agree with you." The people who work closely with me have fondly called me a "nice bitch" because they couldn't think of another word to describe a woman who gets things done without being hateful. I've also been called a "boss bitch" as a compliment. In fact, when I asked Wade and our younger son what they thought I should title my book, they looked at each other and simultaneously said, "Something with the b-word."

That caught me off guard. "What? Why?"

"That's kinda what you are, but in a nice way," said my husband while holding a pillow up to protect himself.

Wade knows better at this point. One time, when we were newly married, we had an argument over the phone when he said, "I feel like calling you a bitch." I promptly hung up on him. He immediately called me back and told me, "I said I *feel* like calling you one. I didn't call you one!"

Still, the more I thought about using the word *bitch* in the title of my book, the less comfortable I was with it. For one, I'm not a cusser. Well, I sorta am. What I mean is that I'm an internal cusser, which means that I cuss in my head. A lot. I was raised to believe cuss words were reserved for epic "LMS" moments (LMS stands for "lose my stuff," though it can always be replaced by that other, less Southern, s-word). I have literally been known to say, "Do you see how mad I am? I'm cussing!"

I have a friend who is a prolific cusser. She loves it and has literally told me, "I love cussing. It's one of my favorite things." She says the b-word like SoCal teenagers say *dude*. But, oh no, not I! I won't even wear the shirt that says, "I love Jesus, but I cuss a little," because I wouldn't want anyone to know that I cuss, even just a little. Simply writing out the word *bitch*, never mind making it the title of my book, makes me uneasy. *What will my church friends think? Dear Lord, what if my nana sees it?*

But the real reason why I decided against using the word *bitch* in the title is that, when the word is spoken by a man toward a woman, it's almost always meant as an insult. As women, we feel pain when that word is used by a man. It's like we're being written off entirely—dehumanized to the point of being an animal that is beneath them. After all, a bitch is a female dog. At least, when you call a man an asshole, it's a reference to a body part that applies to our own species (and to both males and females).

If women are no longer considered people with feelings,

there is an excuse for others to treat us any way they want, as we are "just a bitch." It can be argued that if as women we use that word, we are legitimizing its use to describe other women. Let's not play in the "bitch ditch." We don't want to give the false impression to our male counterparts that it's OK to reduce everything that a woman is to that word.

* * *

Do you remember how you felt the first time you were called a bitch by a man—that moment when you went from being a person to an object of anger?

I was a freshman in high school when it happened to me for the first time, but I remember it as clearly today as if it happened yesterday.

One of the popular upperclassmen in school was hitting on me at the skating rink. He had been giving me attention all night, holding my hand and bringing me into his conversations with the cool older kids. Eventually, when we were sitting alone in the corner, he kissed me. Then, almost immediately, he tried to put his hand down my pants. I pushed away his hand, but he tried again and again until I firmly told him, "No!"

He looked shocked. Then, he stood up and looked down at me with such disgust. With venom in his voice, he said, "Nobody wants you anyway, you stupid bitch."

In the blink of an eye, he went from trying to get in my pants by using flattery to spewing hate at me and making me fear for my safety. Everything about his demeanor changed once I rebuffed him. His true character became evident when he used that word.

He walked away, leaving me sitting in the corner of the skating rink in utter shock. I couldn't decide if I wanted to cry or go kick his ass. It was demeaning, embarrassing, and made a lasting impression on me. More importantly, it taught me how often that word is used during an emotional moment that is brought on by anger. That's why for years I chose not to say the word myself. And I still would never call another woman a bitch in front of a man. It unwittingly plays right into the male ego and fuels the stereotype that a woman is a bitch if she turns down a man or disagrees with the man.

Despite what others may think of me, I don't consider myself a bitch. I consider myself a strong, independent, loving, hardworking, encouraging, fair yet firm, no-nonsense business woman, wife, and mother. I've always prided myself on not having to be a bitch (most often defined in business as demanding and unpleasant) to fit in with the guys in my industry, or to get ahead. Of course, despite my best efforts, I have often been categorized as one.

I believe I am a genuinely kind person. I care about others, and I fight hard for what's right in all settings, including my business. I am driven to do what's best for my company because what's best for my company is best for the employees, who trust me enough to work for my company, and it's what's best for their families, who depend on the company's success. My goal, in every situation, is to find the win-win if at all possible. I don't try to intimidate or belittle others. I make an honest and concerted effort to be respectful of others and of myself. A personal male friend, who just so happens also to be a branding genius, assured me that I could never fit the bitch mold because I didn't have a harsh appearance or sharp features, yet still agreed that I will be viewed as a bitch simply because I can hold my own and make things happen.

What about you? Are you strong-willed and determined to have the best life you can live? Do you stand up and fight for others along the way? If so, have you been labeled a bitch?

LET'S REDEFINE THE WORD *BITCH*

Back in the 1960s when the hippies were at war with the police—maybe when the police were at war with the hippies—the hippies started calling any police officer they saw a "pig." "Look out, there's a pig," etc. It became endemic; the word was known by everyone to be a reference to police, and if you got pulled over for speeding, it was also a word unspoken inside your head. Finally, one department got smart and made a big deal of the word *pig*, saying it was not a term of derogation but an acronym of pride. PIG meant "pride, integrity, guts," as police were brave and helped everyone. Some still called them "pigs" in a malevolent sense, but it gave the police a positive edge. We women can do the same thing—make an intended insult give us a credo for achievement.

I can't pinpoint the time when I first came up with the idea to give the Big Bad B-Word a new meaning. I believe it was sometime in my late teens, because I remember telling my husband what it meant to me shortly after we started dating. And now, twenty years later, whenever I speak to high school and college girls, I use the following acronym, which best describes what *bitch* now means to me:

B – Beautiful

I – Intelligent

T – Talented

C – Creative

H – Hardworking

Let's take back the word *bitch* and redefine it.

B – BEAUTIFUL

We all want to be successful, independent, and look like supermodels. In reality, the only way to maintain our beauty in the eyes of others is to be kind. We've all met that one girl or guy who is good-looking at first sight, but after getting to know the person, their beauty quickly fades as their negative traits shine through. The opposite is true as well. There are those people who just glow because of all the kindness they show others. Long story short: beauty fades, but kindness stays. And you can tweet that!

I used to have a co-worker who looked like she just walked off a fashion runway. Her hair was always perfect, her makeup flawless, and her outfits put together. Even when sans makeup and in workout clothes, she was jaw-droppingly stunning—a natural beauty who was brimming with self-confidence. She wore tight skirts and four-inch heels at a time when women in business wore menswear, trying not to stand out. Oh, and did I mention that she had a great job in media sales and a booming social life? I was just starting my career, and she was ten years older, so naturally, I was mesmerized.

But oh boy, did she turn out to be an ugly person. When we would have lunch, she was always rude to the waitstaff. It was as if she was annoyed that they were checking in on us. She would do the, "OMG, do you see what that woman is wearing?" when we were out in public. She would put down others around her to make herself look better. She would even hide her insults as compliments. She once told me, "I need confidence like you. I mean, you're bigger than me, and you're so confident." No matter how beautiful she was on the outside, her ugly attitude quickly made her very unattractive to those around her. Guess where that got her?

I recently bumped into that former co-worker. Unfortunately, she was just as negative as before. She had stalled out in her sales career and was in the same position as she was when we met twenty years earlier. She was on her third divorce, and her lack of inner beauty was even more evident because of her desperate attempt to look young and sexy. Sadly, because she was more focused on her outward appearance than she was her inner beauty, time had not been kind to her.

Time takes its toll on everyone's outward appearance. But if you practice the graces and seek to manifest inner beauty and to build people, time will bring out your inner beauty and people will recognize it, and that inner beauty can be how people remember you. Think of your grandmother: Is she movie-star beautiful or just the nicest, most caring person you know because of her inner beauty?

TIPS FOR BEING BEAUTIFUL ON THE INSIDE

1. *Look for the good in the world. There is always something to smile about.*

2. *Learn to get comfortable with yourself. You are unique. Learn from others, but never try to be anyone but yourself.*

3. *Always look for the good in others. Even if you can't stand a person, look for one thing positive about them and repeat that. Even if it's that they are "very photogenic."*

4. *Work on you for you. Take a walk and meditate on all the good in life. Talk to a therapist. Join a faith community. Do things that make you a better person and live a happier life.*

Take affirmative steps to be a better person and count your blessings each day. True beauty is when a person is so encouraging and full of joy that they make those around them joyful as well.

That doesn't mean that we forget about our outward appearance. Of course, we need to look presentable and professional and to smell good—we absolutely need to take care of ourselves and present an outward appearance that does not distract from our inner beauty—but you don't have to watch hours of hair and makeup tutorials, or keep up on the latest trends, to look your best. You just need to be well-groomed and dress appropriately.

I can attest to how dressing the part goes a very long way in how you are perceived, because our appearance will often reflect the way we take care of our professional duties. Dress for the job you want and dress for the impression you want to give others. You don't need to max out your credit card to maintain a professional wardrobe. A smile and smiling eyes can trump designer clothes every time. People like dealing with people they like and who they feel like them.

Some of my favorite places to shop are consignment shops and thrift stores. When I travel, I always try to stop at one. I love the unique items I find. Plus, I love the value. There is a local thrift store I frequent that benefits a home for battered women and children. They sell pants for $5 and often have unbelievable deals on brand-new slacks from high-end designers. Even if I have to spend $20 to have them hemmed, that means I spent $25 on a pair of custom-fit slacks that typically go for $195—and I have the inner satisfaction of knowing that my purchase money has gone to help disadvantaged people, not more chrome and mirrors at the mall (THINK INNER BEAUTY).

I don't claim to be a beauty expert, but I can't overstate the power of drinking water and moisturizing. It works wonders. I literally slather on face moisturizer from my forehead to my cleavage every night. Your body NEEDS moisturizing, inside and out. Stay hydrated and use skin care. Period!

TIPS FOR BEING BEAUTIFUL
ON THE OUTSIDE

1. *Shop Sephora online. You can get up to three free samples every time you place an order, and I challenge you to find me one woman who doesn't love free samples.*

2. *Invest in under-eye pads and sheet masks. You can get these for a dollar in some stores. They are my go-to refreshers when I'm working a trade show or traveling.*

3. *Exercise. And don't just exercise to try and get a body you love but use exercise as a stress reliever because* **stress never looks good on anyone.**

4. *Take advantage of local beauty schools. I am a huge fan of going to beauty schools for two reasons. One, I love to help young people grow in their trade. Two, it's cheap! The one I use does facials for $20. I get the same exact treatment as a professional facial, but for a fraction of the cost. Of course, it's not in a private room, and the technicians are still learning, but it's so much better than what I could do myself.*

5. *Smile! RBF (resting bitch face) is a thing. And it's not attractive at all and only reinforces the business bitch stereotype. Make a conscious choice to smile, because it makes a difference in your demeanor, which influences how you're viewed by others. Even if it's just lifting the corners of your mouth while you work, make a choice to have a pleasant look on your face. Don't worry about the lines around your mouth. They disappear when you smile. Remembering to smile will improve your*

mood and the mood of those around you! Also, it's been said it takes more muscles to frown than it does to smile—SMILE!

I – INTELLIGENCE

Some people are born with it. Some people work hard to gain it. Intelligence is not just your IQ or what you know; it's how you turn facts you have gathered into wisdom. When I started my company, I had no idea what I was doing. I wasn't a math whiz or naturally gifted at manufacturing. I had to learn. I had to be resourceful. I had to work hard to understand things that come to naturally to others. And I had to work hard to draw on my natural talents to lead with my strengths.

There are many types of intelligence. Experts calculate maybe as many as a dozen separate types of intelligence: situational intelligence, emotional intelligence, and business intelligence to name just a few.

Let's talk about emotional intelligence (referred to as EQ, or emotional quotient). Even though I don't believe managing EQ is an issue strictly for women, it's something we have to pay extra attention to, given the stereotype that women in business are emotional and take things personally. For example, how do you react when you're upset about something, and a man asks you, "Is it that time of the month?" Tell me that doesn't evoke an emotional response. But emotional intelligence is more than just controlling an outburst. Emotional intelligence often determines our success and happiness in life. I highly suggest researching EQ.

One of the best books I've read on this subject is *Emotional Intelligence 2.0* by Travis Bradberry and Jean Greaves.

Understanding why we do certain things and the emotions behind our actions will help us navigate the world and be more successful in male-dominated industries where one of us may "represent" all of us, at least for the foreseeable future.

One of the best examples I can think of occurred when I was stood up by a high-end stylist I had hired to do my hair and makeup for an event at which I was being honored. That event was a critical part of my public brand, so I needed to look my best and be camera ready. The guy didn't show up at all, which left me with only 45 minutes to do my hair and makeup before I took the stage. After the event, I was livid and let him have it over the phone, repeatedly. The incident ate away at me for months. Typically, I'm the type of person who can let things go and move on. If you hurt and disrespect me, I simply take my leave from the relationship or situation as soon as possible. So why was I thinking about what happened with that stylist constantly?

I finally had to ask myself why it bothered me so much. I realized it wasn't because I was stressed out when he didn't show up; it was because I felt that he didn't value me and that I wasn't as important as his other clients. It was the "imposter syndrome" rearing its ugly head. Once I realized why I was so upset, I was able to look at the reality of the situation, which was that he was unprofessional and did not take the service portion of his business as seriously as he should. He told me he didn't put my event down on his calendar, so it slipped his mind. That showed the low value he placed on his work but also made me realize that his actions had nothing to do with me.

Without exercising my emotional intelligence, I would have walked around being bitter. And bitter does not make anyone look better. When something happens in our lives that upset us, we must ask why it bothers us.

The best advice I ever received on this topic is something called the "5 Year Rule." If it's not going to matter in five years, don't spend more than five minutes being mad about it.

Improving and getting more in touch with our emotional intelligence is part of the equation, and the other part is working on our business intelligence. Be a student of business and life. I am always listening to audiobooks and taking leadership classes. Any class the Small Business Administration offers, I take. I take classes at my local college and innovation hub. I attend a speaking series that features leaders who have come before me and have done more than I have (so far). I even listen to leaders in different industries. I love the podcast Shrimp Tank. It interviews people who have been successful in many different areas. I'm continually striving to learn more, and that includes learning from those I work with every day. They have new fresh ideas. They may know of a new technology or a new program with which I'm familiar.

As soon as I start to think I know everything, my career is doomed, so I'm always learning and always asking questions. I'm a lifelong student—my brain power is part of my "beauty"!

T – TALENTED

Yes, you are talented!

Talent is something we tend to think only comes in the world of art or sports. No one ever says, "She is so talented at business." But in fact, being good at business is a talent. Think of how many talented artists and athletes end up broke because they have absolutely no business talent. Being good at business is a learned skill.

How many of you have ever had to perform in a talent show and been at a loss for what to do? That happened to me once. I was in a leadership class, and we had a talent show that everyone was required to participate in. I am the first to admit that I have no easily performable talents. So I ended up giving business and life advice as my talent. I wrote down questions from the audience and answered them for a full five minutes as my talent. Hearing those questions and being able to provide answers reinforced to me that business is definitely a talent—and a talent I had.

Everyone has a talent. You just have to know where to look for it. Teachers have a knack for public speaking. They regularly speak in front of large groups of people, which is not easy. Consider that most people fear public speaking more than anything else in the world—some even more than death. Some people would literally rather die than speak in front of a group of people, yet teachers do it every day. That is a talent. Accounting is a talent, and one I am grateful other people have. I can take the pulse of a business and gauge by the financials whether or not that business is healthy, but I don't have a knack for everyday accounting, which is why I am so grateful that many of the people I work with do have that talent (you can hire people who have skills you don't have).

Never doubt that you have talent. You can refer to it as a skill or passion, but recognize it as a talent, nonetheless. Identify your talent and work tirelessly to improve it.

"Do the thing you fear most and the death of fear is certain."
—MARK TWAIN

C – CREATIVE

Creative doesn't necessarily mean crafty or artistic. I don't have a single crafty bone in my body. I once attended a women's event that included a DIY guided class on how to make a coaster out of a piece of tile, fabric, and some spray glue stuff. There was somebody standing over me explaining the steps and telling me what to do. I had a room full of well-meaning women cheering me on, and I still messed it up. My coaster was the only one with a wrinkle in the fabric. Not one crafty bone!

What I mean by being creative is more about how to make a space for yourself in the world, personally and professionally. Many women do not have the privilege of legitimate business connections. They either didn't grow up in a family that had connections, and, even if they did, they are seen as someone's daughter who is all grown up now. I've seen women whose parents were well connected, either in business or government, and still must fight to be seen as viable businesswomen. Those women are often invited to the social reception, but not into the boardroom.

I remember receiving a phone call from the daughter of a high-ranking government official who was 12 years my senior. She called for advice on how to grow her business to the next level. She was a woman who literally had access to the CEOs of Walmart, Tyson, and J. B. Hunt. And those are only the ones that I was aware of. She sat at tables with these CEOs at social events and spent a lot of time with them when they were around her father, but when she approached them about business advice, she was blown off. When she asked one of those CEOs to be her mentor, she was told, "You can learn a lot more from your mother." Although a great woman in her own right, her mom was a school librarian for 30 years.

As those without certain privileges and connections, we have to be creative in creating a space for ourselves. One idea is to join a local networking and business advocacy group, such as your local and state chamber of commerce or various industry trade groups. Make it a point to meet successful people in your field. If there is a networking reception, go and network. You can't be shy when it comes to building your network. Everyone moves around at the events, shaking hands and introducing themselves. I promise that you won't look weird. These events are made for awkward introductions.

Ask for help. If you meet someone who could be helpful, ask for their opinion on your project. Ask if they know whom you should speak with about your career, or a sale you are trying to make. Business people understand that deals are made through connections. I'm not talking about being a social ladder climber. Be honest and genuine, but also not afraid to ask for help. An academic study was conducted years ago asking business school graduates how they ended up in the job they were in: 69 percent said they obtained their job through friends or family. You can't choose your family, but you can make your own friends.

Seek out a mentor, or a sponsor, which is a mentor who puts their support for you into action. Find someone who has achieved the success you wish to accomplish and simply ask them to work with you, mentor you, or sponsor you. You will be shocked at how many people are honored to be asked and will gladly say yes. For years, women have complained about a lack of female mentors in their fields. As the tide turns, and more of those women are becoming seasoned professionals, they are more than happy to mentor a woman on the rise. And you—BE A MENTOR! No matter your position, there is always someone who can learn from you, someone who desperately would be grateful for a little nurture, wisdom, and an ally.

Find both female and male allies, and if you can't find any, then work to create some. Allies are people who genuinely have your best interests at heart. They can introduce you to the people you need to know and give you credibility based on their recommendation of you. My allies and I may not hang out socially, but I know they will help put me in spaces that can advance my career.

Dr. Teri Cox of Cox Communications once explained to me that there are people who are "with you," and people who are "for you." "With you" people are those who are with you in the moment. They may be acquaintances, co-workers, or sometimes even "frenemies," but they don't support you when you are not around. "For you" people may not be the ones you hang out with on a Friday night, but they are the ones who will promote you and open doors for you. They want what's best *for* you. Find some "for you" people, because they will be the allies and mentors who will help you open the doors you're supposed to enter.

Being creative is how I built my network and funded my business. It has made all the difference between failure and success for me. I tell everyone, "I'm nothing if not creative and resourceful!"

H – HARDWORKING

In today's social media-obsessed world, it's easy to be fooled by posts from people with a million followers "living the life" while trying to be motivational entrepreneurs.

Let me drop this truth on you: Success in business isn't based on how many followers you have. It's based on how many paying customers you have. And to take it to a deeper level, it's based on how much profit you have, and in my personal opinion, how much good you do. I have seen many businesses go under because the person was more concerned with the appearance of success than actually building a customer base or product line.

Everyone today seems to think that they *are* their brand. I once heard a woman stand up at an entrepreneurs' conference and say she needed help growing her house cleaning business. She needed help on branding, then said, "I am my brand." No dear, you're not your brand. A clean house is your brand. People are not going to see selfies of you on Instagram and hire you to clean their house. They want to see before and after photos of homes. You need a memorable tag line and logo, not selfies. But selfies are easier...and thus deceptive as "solutions" to your branding problem.

> You have to put in work.

You have to put in work. I'm talking "up-all-night making product, meeting the next morning, then mowing the yard in high heels while holding a baby on your lap because a customer is coming the next day and you can't afford to pay someone to mow the lawn" hard work. And yes, I actually did that. We had our first big product testing with the Federal Aviation Authority, and we had to remake parts until 2 a.m. The FAA representative was showing up at 8 a.m., and our newest customer was showing up for a 4 p.m. meeting. So, after picking up my son from daycare, I hopped on the lawnmower. He slept in my lap as I mowed the lawn so it would look decent when the customer arrived. Thank God for a riding mower!

There is a saying: *Hard work beats talent when talent fails to work hard.* There is no replacement for hard work. Period.

> *"Genius is 1 percent inspiration and 99 percent perspiration."*
>
> —Thomas Alva Edison

REFLECTION TIME

I have read several yearly devotional journals authored by a multitude of people. When I answer a journal question, I write the year next to my answer. That way when I read it the following year, I can see how far I've come. I invite you to do the same here. After you finish the book, you can pick it up in a year or so and see how far you've come!

1. What about yourself do you find beautiful?
   - Inner

   - Outer

2. What do you want to improve?
   - Inner

   - Outer

3. What are your intellectual strengths? What do you want to improve?

4. What is your talent? What comes easy to you that others find difficult?

5. Where can you get creative to open a space for yourself or your business?

6. Where have you worked hard? Make an inventory of where you have had to work hard. This will come in handy later!

CHAPTER 2

DESTROYING GENDER STEREOTYPES

Are women really being held back by gender? There is a popular theory that suggests women are being held back because of the unconscious bias that exists against women in workplace leadership positions. In other words, before you even interview for a job, someone has already stereotyped and drawn conclusions about you just by the name on your resume.

Here is how it goes: As soon as "Jane Doe" applies for a position, she will have managers secretly wondering if she is of child-bearing age and might become pregnant. If she becomes pregnant, Jane will have to take leave sometime in the near future. What if Jane then decides to stay home with her child and the company has wasted time and money training her?

If Jane already has children, interviewing managers will wonder if she will likely miss work to care for her children when they are sick since moms are stereotypically the primary caregiver. Then, of course, there is a high likelihood that Jane will be emotional and unable to handle herself during difficult negotiations. If Jane makes it to the interviewing process because she is middle-aged, has no children and is non-emotional, chances are that she has an attitude and thinks she's all that.

It's this type of stereotyping that leads people to assume that John Doe would have the edge over Jane, even if they have the exact same qualifications. There is even more stereotyping when the female applicant has a name with an ethnic (read non-white) American sound to it. Where John Doe has the advantage over Jane Doe, both have the advantage over Ja'Nae Doe. I have seen this time and time again as I have sat with company leaders as they try to find qualified applicants to fill leadership roles in their organizations.

In her research on women in leadership, Dr. Eva Fast, professor of business at John Brown University, says the following in regards to the danger of stereotypes, "One of the most widely discussed phenomena, which seeks to explain the gap in our understanding of this issue, is whether the determination of women's effectiveness as leaders is rooted in real behavioral differences or a perception reinforced by harmful stereotypes which became reality."

STEREOTYPE:
WOMEN ARE EMOTIONAL

"I don't think you should be involved in this meeting. You are too emotional about the subject."

That was the statement made by a male board member to Savannah, a female CEO, regarding the board's hiring of a consultant who had once sexually harassed her when they were co-workers at another company. Savannah had endured more than 18 months of the consultant grooming her. He gave her the spotlight in their presentations and gained her trust, but pretty soon, he started putting his hand on her knee all while giving her the "female tasks" during their project. Not long after that, the consultant started discussing his sexual activities with her.

As Savannah became more and more uncomfortable, she made it a point to tell him that she was in a relationship and some of his behavior made her uneasy. The next time he put his hand on her lower back, she told him, "I'm not a fan of people other than my boyfriend touching me." It got so bad that she made it a point to have her boyfriend bring her dinner at the office when they had to work late, but that only made things worse.

The consultant went from being inappropriate to downright demeaning. He diminished her work to fellow employees and disrespected her in front of clients. When he sent her a particularly hateful email, she forwarded it to her boss at the company where they both worked at the time, but his only response was, "I can't make him stop being an asshole." Savannah eventually left the company.

Once she had established herself as the CEO at a different company, Savannah made sure that her board knew that she had been previously harassed, without getting emotional about it. She wanted to make sure that she was honest from the start. When the possibility came up for this same employee to be hired in the company she was now the leader of, she stepped up and shared her experiential knowledge of his harassing conduct and the hostile work environment he had created at the company where they had been co-workers. She disclosed that information in her original statement to her company's board of directors, as they were contemplating hiring the cad. Savannah didn't raise her voice, nor did she cry.

It didn't matter. Even after explaining with directness in a clear-cut email that hiring the man as a consultant after learning that he had harassed her at another company was a complete insult to her as the CEO and could possibly tarnish the company's reputation, she was still labeled as emotional (despite having the email reviewed by other leaders to ensure she wasn't including any "emotional verbiage"). She just included the evidence and a statement. So why did the email still come off to the board as being too emotional?

Because the male member read it with bias. He just assumed in his head that she was speaking in an emotional tone because she discussed something that would, understandably, evoke an emotional response. Women are emotional. How many times have we heard that before? That is not just an old school stereotype.

* * *

In 2018, when my son was a freshman in high school, he told me about a debate with another male student. They argued over the idea that women were not capable of running companies because, as the other young man put it, "they are slaves to their menstrual cycles, and once a month they would make emotional business decisions." Luckily my son could call on his mother, who runs a successful international company, as an example to the contrary.

Undeniably, there is gender bias in the workplace. It's well documented, researched, and debated everywhere from 24-hour news channels, to blogs, and in college courses across the country. Also undeniable is the fact that men and women are different. Personally, I believe that the "women are emotional" stereotype comes from how many (not all) women tend to be less compartmentalized than most, if not all, men. I once heard a pastor describe it as follows: "Men are like waffles. Each square holds its amount of syrup, and they don't touch the square next to it. Women are like spaghetti. Everything flows and touches everything else." Upon further research, I found there is even a book titled *Men are Like Waffles and Women are Like Spaghetti* by Bill and Pam Farrel.

Stereotypically speaking, men also tend to take less personal responsibility for the actions of others than women do. When their child misbehaves, men are more likely to wonder, *What's wrong with my child?* A woman in that exact same situation is more likely to wonder, *What's wrong with me as a mother?* or, *Where did I go wrong when raising my child?*

Because they are socialized to be more focused on relationships and feelings, women tend to personalize almost everything. Usually, when a woman becomes emotional, as men would say, it's because of many things building up— inside the workplace and out—which can be a disastrous combination. I've heard of women having tearful breakdowns in bathrooms and boardrooms, and I too have experienced my fair share of "emotional" moments. In fairness, if as a woman, I am aware of such moments, it can be no surprise men would remember them as well and think of them as aberrant or less that optimal conduct, thus the stereotypes.

One such moment occurred while I was participating in a leadership class that consisted of industry leaders from all over my home state of Arkansas. During the class, we attended seminars in different cities and towns throughout the state to learn about different industries and communities. Before the seminar, I had a whirlwind week, traveling to three different states in seven days. I went from a work trip in Boston to see my ill father in Dallas, Texas, and then directly to the leadership seminar to learn about the Arkansas forestry industry. Those seminars generally lasted two and a half days. They began at 7:30 a.m. and ended around 10 p.m., which made for a long workday.

Given the subject matter and nature of the seminar, we had to spend many hours outside in the heat and humidity. For those of you who haven't experienced summer in Arkansas, imagine walking through a fog where you can feel the hot, wet air as it wraps around your body, causing you to sweat instantly. Add that to walking around in the woods with bugs, possible poison ivy, snakes, and, worst of all, chiggers (tiny bugs that attach themselves to your skin and leave you itching for days). I am confident they come straight from hell. I was physically and emotionally exhausted.

On the second day of the seminar, I received a text from Alicia, a young woman who had been in my care as a pseudo foster child during her teen years. I cared deeply for Alicia, as I had helped her through a very tough time in her life years earlier. She called to tell me that she needed my prayers because she had been sexually assaulted. A few hours later I learned that my nineteen-year-old son decided to move out of my home, without discussing it with me first, and move in with his girlfriend. Needless to say, I felt that the decision would not lead anywhere good.

To make matters worse, the evening agenda was shifted at the last minute, leaving about half the class sitting around for an hour waiting for the next session to start. My frustrations grew as I pictured all of my work piling up back home while I sat there being unproductive. I imagined my family and friends falling apart at the seams while I was waiting for the evening session to begin.

Once the session finally started, it happened. As a classmate was presenting to the group, a couple of women walked in an hour later than the agenda said we were to begin. Their giggling unintentionally interrupted my classmate. That was the last straw! I flew out of my seat and, with my finger pointed at the door, screamed, "Get out!" I was so filled with anger and hurt that I got right up in the face of one of the women, Jennifer, and yelled at the top of my lungs as if she were the cause of all my frustration.

And I didn't stop there. I actually stood guard outside the door, mean-mugging the other late-comer classmates and telling them to quietly enter through the back door, as if I were an evil nun from a Catholic school in a 1970s horror movie.

I didn't return to the session that night (which must have left my classmates thinking that I had lost my mind) and went straight to my hotel room. It was an epic "emotional" meltdown moment. I looked like an absolute lunatic in front of some of the most prominent business leaders in the state. Great! Now I was the crazy, emotional bitch. How was I going to recover from that? And of course, I happened to unleash my tornado of crazy on Jennifer, who is one of the sweetest, most kindhearted women I have met. Under any scenario, she was completely undeserving of my wrath. I can't even imagine what both the men and women said afterward.

It was beyond embarrassing, and I beat myself up over losing my cool the entire night. I couldn't sleep. I just kept replaying the incident in my mind. *Why couldn't I keep it together? Why did I have to be so emotional? How on earth could I LMS (lose my stuff) in that situation?* I felt like a total and complete failure. Surely my classmates thought I was a fraud—just another emotional female who couldn't remain composed in a professional setting. As if it couldn't get any worse, I had to get up and speak in front of the entire group the following day.

HOW TO COMBAT THE "TOO EMOTIONAL" STEREOTYPE

1. DON'T IGNORE YOUR FEELINGS. FACE THEM.

The day after my outburst on poor unsuspecting Jennifer, I quickly apologized to her and tried to move on. I was not proud of my actions, and I wish I had better control of my emotions, but it happened. I put on my "business face" and pretended that all of the emotionally stressful noise in the background wasn't happening as I got up to make my presentation. I buried my feelings and focused on the task at hand as if nothing was wrong, but it didn't entirely work because I was still on edge. A kind word from another classmate sent me to the bathroom in tears.

The problem was that I never allowed myself time to acknowledge my feelings. I should have taken an inventory of why I was upset and been honest about where the feelings were coming from. Once you are honest about your feelings, you can remove the emotions of outside influences from the business at hand.

> I never allowed myself time to acknowledge my feelings.

2. TAKE A MOMENT.

It's perfectly OK to excuse yourself from a work situation so you can gather your thoughts. Decide for yourself which action will allow you the room to think most clearly. For some, a few deep breaths are enough. For others, simply listening and sitting still is enough. Others might take time away, either the day off or just a few minutes alone in a quite space. The crucial thing is to remind yourself that what happens at work, or in business, is entirely separate from whatever is going on outside of work. When in doubt, compartmentalize.

On the night of my outburst, I knew what I was thinking about and where my mind was before I ever went into that room. I could have excused myself from the seminar and avoided the situation entirely. Or, I could have taken a moment to write down how I felt. I could have called one of the trusted members of my tribe and tried to decompress.

3. EXPRESS YOURSELF.

After you have acknowledged your feelings and gathered yourself, be honest. If you are still rattled, it's perfectly OK to tell people, "I've had a tough day with some personal issues, and I'm concerned that I may not be in the best position to deal with this work issue at the moment. I would like to resume this discussion later, and I will get back to you by close of business with a response."

If the first two steps don't bring you back into focus on the task at hand, this is a great option. It clarifies for others with a clear and reasonable explanation as to why you plan to regroup, and also assures them that you will complete the task promptly. Don't leave it open-ended; make it a point to provide a reasonable and comfortable timeline of when the task will be complete or when you will pick up the conversation.

WHEN THE TEARS START FLOWING

From a young age, girls are socialized to believe that crying is the way to express frustration while boys are taught to resort to anger and frustration. Since women have not been prevalent in the workforce for very long—and continue to strive for equal representation—it's not surprising that crying at work is frowned upon and becomes the subject of gossip. When a man yells or cusses, it's never discussed again, or if it is, it might even be discussed with reverence. But here's the truth: Some people are criers. It will happen for some women, no matter what.

Just like you don't want to use profanity in the workplace, you also don't want to cry, but guess what? It happens! If you feel it coming on, follow the three steps listed above. If the tears start flowing, own it just like you would an accidental outburst of profanity. Then, keep going. You haven't ruined your career, and you can recover. Feel free to say something like, "Thank you for understanding how upset I am," and then just move on like it never happened. Bad times can even build closer relationships; it's been proven that asking someone to help you is an excellent way to start a friendship.

As allies, if you happen to be in the room when another woman bursts into tears, please, for the love of everything good, don't reach over and hug her! That just draws more attention and makes it worse. Wait until after the issue has been resolved to let her know that you empathize with her and offer a word of encouragement. Don't draw attention to the crying. Nobody wants that. Remember, queens fix the crowns of other queens in private. If you have the opportunity to redirect the conversation, then do so. If you can't, then allow your colleague to handle it the way she sees best and support her offline.

WHEN YOU ARE ON THE RECEIVING END

If you are ever on the receiving end of a tornado of crazy, I beg you to be a Jennifer. When I unleashed my crazy on Jennifer, she was upset, and she told me so. But when she saw me the next day, she behaved with such grace. She was kind and forgiving. She didn't dismiss me as a crazy, bossy-ass bitch, and she didn't hold onto the hurt that I caused her. She just walked by, gave me a smile, and put an understanding hand on my shoulder for a couple of seconds. That meant a lot to me. I sent her a thank-you text, and we've actually built a great friendship since the incident.

Now, getting back to what I like to refer to as LMS… (Remember "lose my stuff"?) Just as you may LMS, it's just as likely that you will be the one with a chance to show grace to someone else if you find yourself on the receiving end of a tornado of crazy. When the moment comes for you to straighten the crown of another queen, be like Jennifer. Gratitude for another's kindness is a great way to build a closer relationship.

"SHE'S EMOTIONAL. HE'S PASSIONATE."

Have you heard this one before?

The expression of emotion has historically been labeled differently between the sexes. Working in a predominately male environment, I have seen plenty of men have emotional moments, including throwing what could only be described as downright temper tantrums. Yet, when they explode, it's referred to as "losing their cool," but a woman in the same situation is said to have gotten "all emotional" about it. I heard those direct quotes from male managers regarding two separate emotional interactions with employees, one male and one female, within the same week.

An excellent example of that same bias in the media occurred in 2018 when champion tennis player Serena Williams had a verbal altercation with a chair referee, Carlos Ramos, calling him a "liar and a thief" because of penalties she received during the game. She did not scream, nor did she cry, but she was clearly upset with him and spoke with authority. After she made the statement, Williams was given a game penalty, which would result in her losing the U.S. Open.

After the match, Serena pointed out to the judging authorities that men had made many statements to referees that were much worse and had not received game penalties. In fact, in 2017 a male tennis player named Novak Djokovic got into a heated argument with Ramos, yelling and cursing at him. At one point, Djokovic stated: "You're losing your mind" and accused Ramos of having a double standard. Djokovic received no penalty for his actions toward Ramos.

There has been much debate and division over these instances in the tennis world. Not being a tennis buff, I will not speak to whether Ramos followed the rules of tennis equally between the sexes or not. However, regardless of how Ramos chose to enforce the rules with each of the two players, the way the media headlines read after each occurrence showed how the general public labels outbursts differently between the two sexes. Compare "Novak Gets into a Heated Argument with Chair Ump" to Serena's headlines. USA Today's wrote, "Serena Williams Has Another U.S. Open Meltdown, Clashes with Ump" while The Daily Caller's headline read, "Williams Explodes after U.S. Open Dispute with Ump."

I have dealt with this on a personal level as well. I had been invited to be part of a group of business owners who would meet with our state representatives and senators to have an open discussion about the business climate in our state. I was nervous. We met at one of the best hotels in the city, and when I walked into a massive conference room to see 34 business owners sitting around the giant U-shaped table, I couldn't help but notice that there were only two other women.

One at a time, each official stood up at the table to speak. Time stood still while I waited my turn. When I was finally called upon, I stood up and instantly felt every single eye on the place bearing down on me. I held it together and spoke with clarity and confidence when providing a high-level explanation of my company and asked if there was any possibility of bringing back a state-sponsored health insurance plan for small businesses. I explained how my company benefited greatly from that discontinued insurance program and how I found it hard to find reasonably priced health insurance after the discontinuation of the program.

Suddenly, the moderator attempted to quiet me. He left his podium and began to walk in front of me. I jokingly said, "Don't play my Grammy music, I'm almost done."

I finished my statement with the moderator standing in front of me, staring me down. He had not mentioned a time limit, nor had he asked me to wrap up my statement before moving toward me. As a matter of fact, he had not said anything before making his way to stand in front of me. His behavior alone was demoralizing. To make matters worse, after I was done, the moderator stated that he would not tolerate emotional outbursts during the meeting. Emotional outbursts? Nothing I said was emotional, but I let it go.

The next man to speak began to yell and point at the elected officials. He asked a total of four questions and became more heated with each one. Not a word was said to him. Not. A. Word. Nobody tried to protect the legislators from his outburst. Instead, the moderator stood firmly in his position behind the podium in complete silence. At one point, another official even looked over to the moderator as if to say, *Are you going to stop this man?*

Yet, I was the one chastised for having an emotional outburst. After the meeting, one of the other women in the room came up to me and said, "He wouldn't have done that to a man."

If you find that you have been labeled as emotional when that is not the case, call it out. Feel free to say, "I am not emotional. My emotions are under control. I will say that I am passionate about this subject."

Lori, a friend of mine, had a similar experience, but the person who shushed her was a woman, which only added insult to injury. The context was a contentious conference call between several companies trying to renegotiate a contract that was expiring after five years in place. The only person who had been around during the prior negotiations was my friend, who was coincidentally also a lawyer.

One of the lawyers representing the other company suggested letting the contract expire, since her client did not see any value in extending it further. Allowing the contract to expire would be against the best interest of Lori's company. Lori reminded the attorney that the contract only had an expiration date because there was the possibility of the agreement being terminated by a regulatory body for matters outside Lori's company's control. She also indicated that she did not appreciate being asked to walk away from a deal that the attorney's client had benefited from so greatly during the past five years.

In response, the attorney said, "Well, I'm sorry you feel that way, but let's not get all emotional about it." Although furious, Lori remained calm and simply replied, "This is not about my feelings, it's about facts. This is a business matter and we would be better off focused on that." This happened on a conference call where Lori and the woman who called her emotional were the only females involved. The men remained silent. I can only imagine what was going through their minds as they listened to a female attorney belittled another female attorney.

While it's frustrating enough to be labeled "emotional" by men, it's maddening to be called emotional by other women. Be mindful not to call other women emotional in front of men. In order to combat the stereotype, we must stop perpetrating the stereotype. As women, while we have no duty to ignore poor performance regardless of the gender of the person involved, we do need to be aware that our comments about other women, especially to or in the presence of men, continue to reinforce the stereotype or feed into confirmation bias.

STEREOTYPE: YOU'RE JUST A PRETTY FACE

"I see why they made you the company representative," said Ted, the smiling quality systems auditor, as he peered at me over his wire-rim glasses.

I was 27-years old at the time and just one year into running my own manufacturing company. It was my very first audit for a quality system that I had worked countless hours planning and implementing within my company. "I am the company representative because I'm the owner of the company and have taken great pride in putting the system in place," I told him.

"Oh well," he said. "Sometimes companies will put the cute secretary as the company rep, thinking it will sway the auditor in their favor."

Ted went on to behave as if my young age, blonde hair, and blue eyes had gotten me to my current position and not my skill set. Ted never lost his smile and clearly was not picking up on my irritation.

Even at this early stage in my career, I was already used to the assumptions. Here are some of my favorites:

- While my husband and I were at a supplier open house to look at purchasing machinery, the salesman cheerfully quipped, "Oh, he let you out of the office for some free lunch, huh?"

- One day, the rudest, most clueless salesmen I had ever encountered walked right past me as I was sitting at my desk and straight onto our factory floor. He was on our manufacturing floor less than a minute before being directed back to me by our production manager. "So, I hear you're the one with the checkbook!" he said—not even giving me enough respect to treat me like the secretary. Or maybe he thought I was the secretary and he was just sexist, so he completely ignored me because he assumed that he could walk right past a woman at a manufacturing company.

- "You must be in marketing?" That's always a good one. What does that even mean? I hear that at trade shows all the time. I suppose they expect a woman who works in manufacturing to show up wearing Dickies and boots instead of a dress and heels.

- "What are you doing down here? You're going to get dirty." I've heard that from some new male employees while I was working on the production floor of my own company. Once, when I was running a machine on the floor, one poor new guy came over to check my work and said to me, "You need to be careful, these machines are expensive," to which I replied, "I know. I wrote the check for them."

I can provide countless examples where people assumed that I was in the position I was in because I was young and cute. And when you're 27, you don't always know what to do. Those types of situations put me on edge, and sometimes I lashed out and jumped all over people who made comments that insinuated I was just a pretty face or a figurehead.

Once, when a male associate in my industry called me "sunshine," I jumped all over him. "Did you just call me sunshine? Do I look like your granddaughter?"

Responding with anger was not the best approach, and it did not win me any respect either. In fact, I learned real quickly that there was no better way to be labeled a bitch than to jump all over a man for a microaggression. Check out "How to Combat the Stereotypes" at the end of the chapter for ways to combat stereotype about women.

THE TOKEN FEMALE

"You were recommended to us by a past guest, and we believe that your presence will greatly raise the estrogen level of our show."

That was the opening line of an email I received, inviting me to speak on Shrimp Tank, a national business podcast. It didn't bother me at all! I actually thanked the host for being intentionally inclusive and doing so with humor. I have been the only female on many boards and industry speaker panels. And I don't mind it. As a matter of fact, I am grateful for it. Seeing women front and center in a male-dominated field will normalize the idea across the industry. Not only that, it will let other women and young girls know that there is a place for them in that field.

A token female is a woman who is selected or hired for the symbolism, or in other words, specifically because she is female. There was a time when tokenism was necessary to place women in positions of authority because, left to their own devices, men were not going to let them in under any other circumstances. The good news for all of us is that those first token females used their positions to forge a path for the rest of us. Now, we can earn a position because we're good at what we do, and we're qualified to do it.

Recently, on a flight to Miami, I happened to find myself sitting next to Amy Rickman, the first female Senior District Manager at Pfizer across all divisions. She went on to reinvent herself in the insurance world. We talked the entire flight, and she told me, "I was a token female for years and was so glad about that. I got a chance that 95 percent of women in 1981 could not get. I made money. Money is independence. Most women did not have that. They were tied to their husband's finances. I was able to ensure my children went to any college they could get in to, no scholarships."

What I (and most women around the world) do not like is someone assuming I got my position simply because I am female. That implies that I am not qualified. Small-minded people may say, "Oh, they needed a woman to fill a quota, so she got the job."

It has been proven that diversity in all facets—race, gender, age, and background—makes a company more successful. Studies have shown that companies with high percentages of females in management or C-suite positions have greater profitability.

A study conducted by the University of California Davis followed 400 companies for 11 years. The UC Davis study reported that the top 25 companies with the highest concentration in female leadership had a median of 4.4 percent return on assets, and a 12.2 percent return on equity in comparison to companies with less female leadership who had returns of 1.9 percent and 7 percent respectively. Similar research results were seen in European countries with laws in place to mandate that certain percentages of leadership positions must be held by females.

Despite the research, many still believe that women are placed in leadership positions as tokens. This idea spawns from laws such as affirmative action, which was put into place in the 1980s in the United States. The idea was to give women and people of color an opportunity to succeed like their white male counterparts. Unfortunately, people do not like to be forced to conform. And those well-intentioned efforts unwittingly spawned the belief that companies were just putting any woman or person of color into positions not because of work experience or educational merit but merely to fill a mandated hiring quota, bypassing better qualified males. The same complaint has been litigated concerning college and law school admissions quotas.

In my experience, women and minorities must work harder to get positions within predominantly white male companies. I have heard executives and department heads say things such as "the applicant must fit into our culture." If you have a culture of all white twentysomething males who play disc golf together on their lunch, it's not likely they will hire a 45-year-old Hispanic female to join their engineering company. It's human nature to go with what you know. Being around others who look like you or have similar life experiences feels more comfortable. Therefore, even today, company boards and C-suite positions in the United States are predominantly held by white males. That's why the saying "If you can see it, you can be it" is so true. The more woman and minorities there are in leadership roles, the more exposure executives have to different people. This breaks downs stereotypes.

Would you hire someone who didn't fit a position, just to fill a spot that "needed" more diversity? I have yet to see someone hire an unqualified person as a token woman or minority. It just doesn't make good business sense. I have seen more people hire family members who weren't qualified, but never a token. Now, is intentional inclusion important? Yes! But don't ever doubt that you were hired for your skill. And these days, thanks to the help of websites such as LinkedIn, you can display your resume for all to see, so it's easier for you to make your experience and qualifications readily available to verify your skill set. I will often request to link with someone who may seem to question my qualifications, knowing full well that they will look at my profile to see if I am indeed qualified. Not only has that eliminated any of their doubts, but it has also opened up many opportunities for me when they needed gender diversity for a project.

HOW TO COMBAT THE STEREOTYPES

So, if jumping all over men for their inaccurate assumptions isn't the way to get respect, what do you do? *Be the best in the room.*

If possible, I would wait until I had the opportunity to dazzle them with my knowledge of industry, machines, and products. I began to enjoy waiting until the men ignored me or spoke down to me just so I could ask them a question they couldn't answer or correct them on a misstated fact. Competence always speaks for itself

You would hope that people would have the decency to treat everyone, male or female, with equal respect. Unfortunately, that is not always the case. If you don't have enough of an online presence to say "GMB" (Google me, buddy) feel free to throw out your qualifications and then follow up by asking, "So, how did you get into this business?" Turn the tables and make them qualify themselves.

Have you ever felt like you were being stereotyped? If I ever feel that I am being stereotyped where I have been placed in the position as the token female or a pretty face, I use the humble brag technique. I casually comment on how long I've been in business or explain my experience with the subject matter.

Don't hesitate to speak up. I always encourage directly calling things out.

I once heard a counterpart at another company try to discredit a female customer. He stated that she didn't know what she was doing and that she only got her job because they "needed someone like her." And by "like her," it seemed clear he was referring to the fact that she was a woman of color. Not only was she the only woman on the manufacturing side of the company, but she was the only person of color on the team for that project. It was at that moment that I understood what it meant to be an ally to women of color. I still smile with pride when I think about the look on that guy's face when I responded by saying, "She's probably so tough because she constantly has to deal with assholes assuming she only got the job because she's a black woman." *Touché.* Needless to say, he never made any more comments like that around me.

Today, I don't reinforce the stereotypes. I don't use statements like, "He's worse than a girl when it comes to gossip or being emotional." I don't say, "You know how woman are" in terms of anything. I removed the phrase, "I don't have female friends because they gossip, cry, and backstab" from my vocabulary. None of that made me seem more relatable to men; it only reinforced the stereotypes against all women. My goal has become to help all womankind, not just myself in the moment.

REFLECTION TIME

Never doubt your skills or potential! You don't need to qualify yourself against the world, but if you need to speak up, do so with confidence. It will not only empower you, but there are others watching you, just waiting for someone to step up and give them the courage to do the same.

1. Have you ever stood up against stereotyping against you or someone else?

2. Is there a time when you didn't stand up against stereotyping? How would you handle that situation today?

3. What can we do to empower others to be courageous?

CHAPTER 3

MEN: THE GOOD, THE BAD, AND THE UGLY

When I was 19 and working in radio, one of the executives made a joke. "You know, what harassment means, don't you? Her ass meant I got in trouble."

I laughed and even retold the joke. I repeat: I was 19. I dealt with harassment so much in my early days that I didn't even know that half of it was harassment. Only when someone got handsy did I actually say something. That happened when my manager at a retail store gave me a shoulder rub and told me that we could "work something out" to save my job. That was a quick and hard no for me.

It was easy to let that part-time college job go, but it was a little different when I was 27. A quality auditor, who was auditing my company on the most critical certification we held, said that I'd score better if I let my hair down. Sadly,

I let my hair down and never said anything to anybody. I distinctly remember feeling so dirty and disappointed with myself that even typing this brings tears to my eyes. I should have said, "I know I'm going to score well because we've worked hard to have an exceptional quality system." Then I should have reported it to the company he worked for and requested he never be sent to audit my company again.

Five years later, I heard that he had been fired because another auditor witnessed him dropping a pencil under the table and looking up a woman's skirt. I wondered how many women had felt dirty and let their hair down during those five years. Have you ever done something against what you believe in an effort to protect what you have worked for?

In recent years, thanks in part to the #MeToo movement, both men and women have become more aware of the lingering effects of sexual harassment, and what it really looks like. I have been blessed to work with and around men who have great respect for women—at least men who have learned what is acceptable behavior in my company and in my presence.

RESPECT ISN'T UNIVERSAL

I was reminded of that overall lack of respect some men have for women after a recent trip to my favorite industry trade show. Something happened that made me immensely proud of my fifteen-year-old son, Noah, and his friend—and even prouder of the fact that Noah is learning, just by living with me, what it means to be a woman in business and an ally to one.

As we were standing in line, a man reached down and grabbed my show badge, which was hanging around my neck, and pressed up against my chest.

"Who do you work for?" he asked.

I proceeded to tell him what I do, what product we offer, and then pointed out that I was there with my son. I made sure to show him how annoyed I was with his actions.

After the man walked off, Noah expressed how angry he was that the man felt it was OK to invade my personal space and grab my badge. I am so proud that my son noticed and took issue with the unacceptable behavior.

"You have no idea what I have to deal with," I told him. "That guy was nothing compared to the guy from last night."

The previous night, I had been at a customer appreciation party hosted by one of our suppliers. The supplier had rented out a swanky restaurant with a live band and multiple bars and food areas. The vibe was much more like a nightclub or afterparty than a traditional networking event. As I was speaking to a colleague, I saw three men look my way. It reminded me of my single days at the clubs when everyone was looking to pick up everyone else.

When I finished my conversation with the male colleague, I walked by the group of three men. One of them stuck his hand out to introduce himself. As I went to shake his hand, he used his strength to pull me into him, so our chests were touching. It was the slimiest move I had seen in a long time. It made me feel dirty and taken advantage of.

Despite how far we have come in business, it still seems to be that the cliché of a woman in a man's world is still the norm. That man clearly wasn't interested in my company or my product. He didn't respect that I was a career woman there for business. He behaved as if I was at some dance club looking for attention.

He asked what I did but didn't listen, then asked if I had a business card.

I said no and walked away. I couldn't wait to get out of there. I felt as if my experience in my field or my position as a business person didn't matter. To him, I was just a woman there who was not to be taken seriously. The whole interaction seemed unreal, and it shook my confidence.

Every single day, women and minorities all over the world will come up against someone who questions the reason they are there. Our biggest weapon against this kind of treatment is to speak up, even when we think we can't.

HOW SHOULD YOU RESPOND?

My son told Wade, my husband, what happened. Wade said to me, "You need to stop being so nice and educate these men that their behavior is not acceptable. They would have never done that to another man." And even if they had, it would have been seen as bullying or harassing and not acceptable with a male unknown to them.

While I knew Wade was right that I *should* have spoken up and said something, the reality was that I didn't feel like I *could*. For Wade, it was so simple, but how do you educate someone about something they don't realize they are doing (and probably have seen done their entire life) without being labeled as a bitch, or risking your job and a possible career opportunity?

When trying to answer that question, I turned to one of my most trusted resources—the internet. I Googled a bunch of different questions about avoiding microaggressions and could not find anything that would have been useful in that situation. No article or blog gave tips to individual women on how to shut down microaggressions based on sex. There was a multitude of blog posts, however, on how to flirt at work, how to shut down a guy that is hitting on you, and how to stop sexual advances in the workplace. Yet, the entire internet appeared devoid of any useful information on how to stop, or even call attention to, the most common microaggressions that women face in the workplace.

Since I wasn't getting any help, I was forced to call upon my experience when developing the following tactics to use if I ever found myself in a similar situation.

1. CALL IT OUT.

Say it like it is. Anyone of the following would work:

- "Why would you invade my personal space and grab my badge?"

- "Grabbing my badge was unnecessary. If you wanted to know my name, I would have told you…if you had given me a chance."

- "Please don't touch my badge."

- "What made you think that it was OK to invade my space and grab my badge?"

2. TURN TO HUMOR.

You can tell a joke and still make the aggressor aware of what he is doing.

- "Well, that was an interesting microaggression! Do you go around grabbing all the girls' badges?

- "So how many men's badges have you grabbed today?"

This tactic is the one I use most often. It gets the point across without blatantly embarrassing the aggressor. It's most effective with men who seem to be ignorant of what they're doing as opposed to the men who continue to use microaggressions even after being made aware of how women feel about it.

I most recently used humor when a young man said that he would ride "bitch" in the company SUV. My response was, "So, if I'm driving, does that mean I'm riding douchebag or asshole? Which microaggressive term do men prefer?"

He responded "asshole," and then asked what I meant. That was an opening to explain how referring to the non-preferred seat as a derogatory term for a woman is like saying that a woman is less than a man. It was clear he had never thought of it that way, and he didn't mean any harm by what he said; he just never realized what he was saying would be insulting to women. I heightened his awareness on that point.

3. RETURN THE FAVOR.

This is a tricky one. In my case, that would mean grabbing that guy's badge right back. You need to be prepared to look like a total bitch to pull this one off without making it look like you're flirting. If I had reached down and grabbed that man's badge, I could have succeeded in making him feel uncomfortable and small, but he could also have taken it as a sign that I was interested in him.

You may want to save this one for microaggressions that are generalized, like when a man asks, "What are you ladies gossiping about?" You could say, "Which sports team are you wasting the company's money talking about? Oh, I'm sorry. I thought we were making overreaching generalizations based on the stereotypes of one's sex." It gets the point across, but also clearly sets a boundary, which, in some cases, is a good thing.

4. REPORT IT!

Tina, an executive at a financial firm and a dear friend of mine, tells a story about how she didn't realize that she had been harassed until the situation was over and she had time to reflect on it. It's an all-too-familiar scenario.

Tina's male colleague in question had initially been incredibly supportive of her. He recommended Tina for her first big opportunity in the world of financial advising and taught her many things in her new position. They had been assigned a significant and exciting project to work on as equals. Tina was eager to do her work with him at first because she felt valued, but she began to notice that she was doing all of the administrative tasks during this joint project. That type of office housekeeping should have been equally shared.

Tina soon began to feel uncomfortable around him as his boundaries around her loosened, and he would put his hand on her waist and continually stand too close for her comfort. When a colleague from another company innocently asked Tina if they were dating, she decided to make it clear to her co-worker that his actions were making her uncomfortable.

After that, his treatment of her changed. He began to demean her in front of employees and customers. Tina took on more administrative work, often working late hours alone. As his behavior became more demeaning and borderline abusive toward her, she took the matter to their CEO, who was male.

The CEO's response, according to Tina, was, "Did you give any signals that you may have been interested in him?" When she told him that she definitely had not, the CEO advised: "Let it blow over. You probably just hurt his pride."

Tina eventually left that company. She didn't make a formal complaint. She didn't note the mistreatment or the concern over his uncomfortable touching during her exit interview.

She later found out that once her colleague left the company, other women were happy to see him go. While he had not been sexually inappropriate with others at the company, he had been demeaning and passed off the administrative work on female co-workers. Tina realized that other women were put in a similar uncomfortable situation because she didn't report what happened during her exit interview.

When harassment or inappropriate behavior goes unreported, it allows those types of manipulative men to move to different companies, where they continue the same behavior. The "Good Ole Boys Club" tends to protect its own, or even worse, they don't see what they're doing as harassment. It's time for the women to form the "Good Girls Club." We must talk to and support one another.

Not reporting that man came back to haunt Tina, because he later came to work as a consultant her new company of which she had been hired as CEO. Tina spoke to her new male partners about the past harassment situation but was told that they couldn't turn him away because she had not made a formal complaint. And since he hadn't harassed her at the current job, there was nothing they could do.

This brings up a related issue. The fact that a female CEO told her male business partners that she was harassed by an applicant should be more than enough reason for them to exclude him from job opportunities. If they trusted Tina to run their company, they should trust her experience with that particular man, no questions asked. Instead, they made the excuse that they didn't want to ruin a man's career over something that wasn't reported or found to be true. Either that was extreme gender bias, thinking that she was overreacting, or the painful truth was they didn't value Tina as much as they valued the man who had harassed her.

Even though it's illegal under federal law, sexual or gender-based harassment in the workplace goes mostly unreported. The U.S. Equal Employment Opportunity Commission, a government agency responsible for processing the sexual harassment complaints that do get reported, estimates that 75 percent of all workplace harassment incidents go unreported altogether. I suspect the reason so many incidents go unreported is that they are not cut-and-dry. When it's not blatant inappropriate contact, or a sexual comment, we're not sure what to do or how to report it.

As business owners and leaders, we need to give people the space to report behavior that makes them uncomfortable. All too often we judge the person who comes forward without looking into the incident. When we don't give people a safe place to come forward, we are giving our stamp of approval to different kinds of harassment.

Whenever a man's behavior raises a red flag for me, I do a little online research. If I am lucky enough to know someone who worked with him previously, I'll ask for an off-the-record opinion of him. I'll even call women he has worked for and ask their personal opinion. That opens the door for them to share their experiences.

If you are completely uncomfortable reporting the person at the time of the harassment, I encourage you to document what you experienced. Write down everything that the harasser did and said, and also write down how you felt. Put that all in an email and send it to yourself. That does two things:

1. It can be very healing for you. Acknowledging that it happened while acknowledging the feelings it caused and working through those feelings can help you understand yourself, and how to heal from the process.

2. It also gives you time-stamped evidence if you ever feel you need to come forward for yourself, or to protect other women.

For the women who end up coming forward years later about the harassment they received from men, this helps to validate their claim. It's sad that victims are not believed without proof. But in a world of possible false reports and gender stereotypes, it helps to have dated proof.

5. NEVER MAKE A FALSE REPORT!

Even if everything in your being tells you that a particular guy is a creep, if he hasn't done anything, don't make a false report.

- It's illegal and immoral.
- It creates a bigger problem for women in the future.

Even worse than not reporting harassment or misconduct is making a false report. This not only ruins your reputation, but it also gives people a reason to excuse legitimate harassment reports in the future. Harassment reports are already a sticky subject to begin with because they are often one person's word against another, but when you create doubt in the minds of those responsible for taking action, it only makes things worse for you, and women in general.

The National Sexual Violence Resource Center found that while false reports make up between 2 and 10 percent of total rape reports, 63 percent of sexual assaults are not reported to authorities. Even though false reports pale in comparison to unreported assaults, women are doubted continuously because of the actions of a few.

Do not make a false report! You are better than that. If someone is belittling you or treating you as if you are less than your male counterparts, report it, but don't embellish or lie at any time.

WHAT CAN WE LEARN FROM MEN?

As a woman in the business world, I have dealt with almost every type of business professional, most of whom are men. As a matter of fact, I cannot think of one single time when I walked into a predominately female-filled conference room, board meeting, or contract negotiation of a for-profit organization. Even within my own company, I am the only female on my executive leadership team. I am working hard to change that, but as of now, that's just a fact. The manufacturing industry, like many others, is overwhelmingly male.

You and I are well aware that as women we bring a different skill set and different ideas to the business world. We can't help but be uniquely female. Most women's ability to empathize, multitask, and exercise emotional intelligence far outweighs our male co-workers. Yet, with all our unique qualities, and despite being 52 percent of the professional working population, women make up less than 14 percent of the executives in Fortune 500 companies. We need books like this. We need blogs that advise us on how to make it a man's world. So, what do we do next?

If our male counterparts are still running the companies that produce most of the world's wealth and employment opportunities, we need to learn from them. Yes, we are different, even better in some ways, but we limit ourselves when we do not take advantage of the resources around us. And guess what? Male executives can be a huge resource. So, let's take advantage

> Learn from a man, act like a lady, and lead like a boss.

of the male-dominated world and learn from them. You've heard the saying "Think like a man, act like a lady." Well, let me introduce you to a new saying:

Learn from a man, act like a lady, and lead like a boss.

BOARDROOM BULLIES

More than once I have been appointed to a state agency board of directors. Being appointed by the governor to sit on a state agency board meant that I would be one the people who were charged with overseeing and running an entire division of state government. Do you know the people who run your state's Department of Transportation or Department of Health? Well, I, among others, had been appointed to ensure they balanced their budget and did their job.

As my time on a particular state board progressed, it became clear that I was one of the few board members who had actually researched and used the programs at the agency we were appointed to govern. That gave me a distinct advantage, an advantage not granted to me because of my age, sex, family connections, or work experience. That advantage had nothing to do with the success of my company. I had that advantage because I was resourceful. Years earlier, when times were tough in business, I focused on finding resources within state agencies that could help me improve my business and find a trained workforce. Using those programs would allow me to help give people an opportunity to better themselves and improve my workforce with the limited economic resources I had at the time.

During a discussion about instituting a new program, I suggested that we use the framework of a state program that was already in place and successful. "We could use the same metrics as the past program. It was easy to understand."

It was a reasonable request, but getting most of my fellow commissioners to hear me proved to be problematic. Initially, I received zero acknowledgement from the rest of the board. I felt as if I were the Holy Spirit whispering in people's ears, even though a big microphone was in front of me so everyone, including the press, could hear.

Finally, one of the male commissioners said, "Maybe we should just keep using the current program. If it ain't broke, don't fix it."

"Sounds like a plan to me," said another male commissioner with a nod.

That went on the entire meeting. I would make a suggestion, then a man would repeat what I had just said, and the other men would agree with him. It was like I was a teleprompter, feeding them lines to recite.

I couldn't believe it. *Is this really happening? Am I going to have to raise my hand so they listen to me? Or worse, start yelling?*

After the meeting, I told the male staffer in charge of the new program at the agency where to find the information, including the applications and reporting documents he had been questioned about, and how to present them. At the follow-up meeting, the staffer presented the documents, but when questioned about them, he could not elaborate.

I sat quietly for a moment and let him stutter. Never once did he say, "Commissioner Radke informed me of where to find the documents and information." After about three minutes of listening to him stumble over what to say, it became clear he had not even researched the current program documents. So I spoke up and explained the process in roughly 30 seconds before proudly sitting back down in my chair.

At that moment, one of the male commissioners said, "Thank you, Don. That's exactly what Mr. Smith and I were asking for."

I. Was. Livid!

It was as if I had not even spoken. As soon as the meeting was over, I had to bolt out of the building. I couldn't take the chance of seeing one of them in the parking lot because I might have run them over with my car, or at least given them a not-so-friendly finger wave! And yes, I am well aware of my need for Jesus, as we say in the South when someone acts in an unflattering manner.

Later that week, during a lunch, I repeated this story to a trusted girlfriend of mine, Dr. Tionna Jenkins. With a knowing look, she said, "Oh, you were mansplained." She went on to tell me about microaggressions. Microaggressions are an indirect, subtle, or unintentional discrimination against members of a marginalized group. Mansplaining is a type of microaggression.

Dr. Jenkins then offered me some advice that would change my boardroom meetings forever. She told me that when a man (or even a woman) tries to reexplain or repeat my statement or idea, just say the following: "Thank you, Mr. Smith. That's exactly what I was saying." Or, "I'm glad you agree with my idea, Mr. Smith."

As simple as that may sound, it took quite a bit of courage for me to use that technique the first time. The very next meeting, the mansplaining started almost immediately. It's funny because I never noticed how often women were mansplained until this form of microaggression was pointed out to me. And it wasn't just me; it was every woman who spoke during the meeting. They were either ignored or mansplained.

After repeating my statement for the third time, I took a deep breath. Fully aware that I was wading into a territory where I might be called a bitch, I calmly stated, "Yes, Mr. Smith, that's my point exactly." Mr. Smith looked at me as if he wasn't sure if I had spoken before and was trying to remember if his statement was an original idea, or if he had heard it from someone else.

Once I began to use the expressions that Dr. Jenkins taught me, the entire conversation within the board meeting changed. Within minutes, I started hearing "I agree with Commissioner Radke's proposal." It felt like sweet vindication! I practically floated out of that meeting. And what's most interesting is that none of my male colleagues on that board have tried to mansplain me since. It was as if I had spoken some magic words that no longer made me invisible to them.

Taking back the power of your own words will change the way others see you. I took this newfound key to communication back to my office and leadership team. Since I work with almost all men, I started to point out their mansplaining. We even noticed sometimes they would mansplain each other! Once after an engineer and a salesman were having a hard time communicating, the salesmen looked at me and said, "Will you mansplain for me?"

I will never forget the moment we were meeting with a supplier who kept repeating my statements to tell me what I *really* meant, and one of my male staff looked at the supplier and said, "Did you just mansplain her?" I almost died. It was wonderful to see the men I work with become aware of this practice.

It's also important to point out that repeating someone's statement back to them to make sure that you understand them is not mansplaining. That's called "active" or "reflective" listening—and it's part of good communication. But repeating someone's thought or idea as if it was your own, that's a version of mansplaining. Mansplaining was popularized by women because of its commonilty

> Repeating someone's thought or idea as if it was your own, that's mansplaining.

in the workplace. However, it's not a male only phenomenon. In my house we also have what we call "momsplaing." This is were I reexplain what my husband just said to my children because I feel they didn't understand and clearly I think I can explain it better.

"I JUST WANT TO…"

In order to stand up to (or conquer) those who consciously or unconsciously try to intimidate, undermine, or ignore us, we need to speak with confidence in order to get the respect we deserve. An interesting phenomenon among women is that we are so concerned with people liking us that it impacts everything we do. We don't want to be too aggressive, too loud, or even just plain "too much." Yet, I noticed that my male colleagues appear to have no concern about being "too much" whatsoever.

As women, we want to assert ourselves, but feel the need to do so politely. We use phrases like, "I just want to express that I believe the best way to spend the budget is this like this." A man might say, "The budget will best be spent this way." Using phrases like, "I want it to be known," "just," "in my opinion," and "I believe," (or worse, "I'm sorry, but…") is like asking somebody to validate your right to have and express an opinion. Those statements also give people permission to dismiss our ideas because we present them as if we ourselves are unsure of their merit and validity.

Pay attention to how you speak in different situations. When you are completely confident in the facts you are presenting, or speaking to your spouse or children, do you use those passive terms? Do you say to your child, "I just believe you should clean your room before you play video games"? No! You say, "Clean your room!" When you are confident in your statement, there is no need to word it in a way that asks for validation.

It's uncomfortable when you try to remove "I just" and "I believe" from your vocabulary. You need to grow accustomed to being uncomfortable in order to become more comfortable with asserting yourself with confidence. It's like starting a new exercise class or trying a new yoga pose. At first, it's incredibly uncomfortable. You feel as if you will never be able to touch your nose to your knee, but if you keep at it, one day you realize it's not uncomfortable anymore. You just bend over and strike the pose with complete confidence. It's the exact same when it comes to speaking with confidence.

So, instead of starting an email with, "I just wanted to let you know about a problem," try writing, "There is an issue with…"

> Why are you using certain words and phrases?

Now, of course, we sometimes use "just" in way that isn't asking for validation. I am not trying to add something else that we as women must police ourselves over. I am encouraging you to ask yourself *why* you are using certain words and phrases. Maybe "just" is your way of really saying, "pretty, pretty, please," or it could be your way of policing yourself from being "too much" when communicating.

When you say something to another person or write an

email, how do you picture yourself? Do you see yourself as a small meek mouse in a room full of tigers, hoping it's OK to speak and be heard without getting eaten alive? If so, then you need to recognize what you are doing—and stop. The subconscious notion that you need to minimize yourself in order to not offend others has you using certain words to soften your statements—not a lack of talent, qualifications, or hard work.

Watch your male colleagues with this in mind. See how you can learn from them. Remember, they don't have any more talent or special skill than you. You can take control of your mind, see it for what it is, and move forward by speaking with confidence.

INTIMIDATION TACTICS

I hate buying a new car. I don't like wheeling and dealing while trying to size up the sales manager to see who gets the upper hand. I am busy. I know what I want, what I'm willing to pay, and I don't have time for the games. Those offices are one of my least favorite places on earth, but there I was, sitting face-to-face with the manager of a local car dealership, trying to finance a company van.

The finance manager showed his displeasure with the deal I had been given. Before going into the dealership, I had used my resources. I contacted a friend in the car industry and asked what the invoice price of the van I wanted was, and he told me that on top of the invoice price, the manufacturer was offering end-of-the-year incentives, and I could get the van for even less than what the dealer had paid for it.

So, I had offered the manager only $250 over what the dealer itself would profit once the manufacturer incentives where applied. Now, he wanted to sell me a warranty and gap insurance. My resource had already informed me that both those products could be purchased for half the offering price.

The manager had already tried to make me feel bad for getting such a good deal. "You know, at the price you're getting, our salesman is only going to make $100 off this sale," he'd said. "That's hard to feed a family on."

As if I should feel bad for getting a good deal.

"Would you like to purchase gap insurance for $1,000? If you would like to go home and discuss it with your husband to make sure he doesn't beat you with a baseball bat, that's fine," he stated in a condescending tone.

"Are you talking to *me*?" I said. "Is that a tactic so I'll make a bad decision to prove my independence from my husband? I'll pay $500 for the gap insurance."

He finished writing the rest of the contract in silence.

One of my favorite ways to deal with people who use intimidation tactics is to question their motives. This takes lots of confidence, courage, and a little bit of IDGAF ("*I don't give a flip*," or whatever f-word you choose to use.) Or, in the situation with the finance manager, plain ole pissed off-ness. I was completely disgusted that he would jokingly use domestic violence as a sales tactic.

Another popular tactic is to stand up and attempt to loom over the other person. I was in a one-on-one meeting with a man who sat across from me at a four-person table inside a conference room. During our conversation, he stood up, stepped over to the corner of the table, and continued to speak while standing over me. I waited for a couple of seconds to see if he was going to sit back down. When it was clear that he wasn't going take his seat again, I asked, "Are you standing up to intimidate me?" He looked shocked and said, "No, I was just stretching." He sat back down, and his entire tone changed.

Let's be real, no one gets up and stands over someone to "stretch." I don't know if it was a conscious decision, or just a natural habit for that man, but he changed his positioning and tone when questioned.

Most of the time when people use intimidation tactics, it's because they are trying to get an advantage, or they feel threatened by your position. And it's plausible that some people don't even realize they are doing it. Whichever is the case, you win by questioning their motives. Secret weapons are only effective if they are kept secret.

> Sometimes, we learn from our counterparts by learning what *not* to do.

I personally don't care to use intimidation tactics. I don't want to win a contract negotiation or debate by belittling someone and making them feel small or uncomfortable. I have, however, learned to disarm someone trying to intimidate me by watching those who use these tactics. Sometimes, we learn from our counterparts by learning what *not* to do.

I had another interaction when the intimidator was a woman who stood over me and tried to use every tactic in the book to get the upper hand. When our discussion became heated, I stood up and tried to move past her. She literally stepped in front of me. This was a woman who held an extremely high position in state government. I remember thinking: *Is this happening? Is she really standing over me trying to intimidate me?* I tried to turn the tables by saying, "What I really enjoyed about the woman who appointed you was that she didn't try to intimidate people or be disrespectful." I didn't change my tone; I let her know that I recognized her behavior and felt that it was unprofessional.

It really bothers me when I think back on that interaction, not because we were both powerful women who each clearly thought the other was in wrong, but because it looked like a catfight to the men watching. It was as if the situation was playing out in slow motion and I could see the men in the room staring at us in shock, awe, and possibly some excitement, waiting to see what was going to happen. In the end, it doesn't matter if the intimidator is a man or a woman—we all must stand our ground and speak with confidence.

On a side note, if you find yourself in a predominately male group meeting, make it a point to sit separately from the other women. This accomplishes numerous things. One, it allows the voices of women to be heard throughout the room. Two, it gives a personal voice as opposed to the two of you being the collective voice of the "women in the meeting." Three, it regulates the men in the room. We all know that we will regulate what we say around certain people. If the women are spread out among their male counterparts during a meeting, it will help them think twice about what they say in mixed company. Diversity is good for all organizations because it makes us think before speaking (for example, if what we are going to say will be offensive to any group members present who might be perceived as "different" from us).

FINDING MALE ALLIES

We have more allies that we think. A male ally is a man who not only uses his influence to promote women in all areas of life, including the workplace, but is a man who draws attention to, and listens to, the women's voices around him. A male ally will point out the microaggressions of other men in his influence as well.

It's important that we let our male colleagues know the struggles we face daily. Making them aware will open their eyes so they can see it for themselves. It doesn't require a passion-filled rant or a formal memo. Simply saying, "Have you noticed that most of the people who don't know me assume that I am not skilled at my job?" Or even, "I want your view on something. The next time we are doing business together, make note if the men only speak to you."

As I grew in the industry, I found male allies who would step up and let others know that I was skilled and knowledgeable in my industry. The salesman who once made the comment about my husband letting me out of the office was met with an answer from his boss, who let him know that I was not only the owner of the company, but I had run every machine on the floor. That was the day that I realized that my reputation in my industry had preceded me. It was a victory!

A good example of this is a man by the name of Rob LaRue. Rob was a quality manager for an international aerospace company who volunteered at a state-wide leadership organization. Rob served as the president of the board of directors when he noticed that there was inequity in the treatment of a female member of the organization named Gemma. After seeing microaggressions in a board meeting, Rob sent an email to the director of the organization, pointing out a number of issues that appeared to be caused by gender bias.

Rob noted that the director had placed Gemma, the only female speaker, last on the board meeting agenda, and then he left before she had the chance to address the board. Rob noted that this caused a chain reaction, and that others left the meeting when Gemma was speaking. Rob plainly pointed out that Gemma had volunteered her time to come to the meeting, and the director should have either stayed, or put her earlier on the agenda if he knew that he was going to have to leave. Then, as the cherry on top, Rob noted, "I have never noticed you leaving board meetings before I speak." Rob included the entire board in the email. He cc'd Gemma as well. I heard about this male ally because Gemma, a friend of mine, was so impressed with Rob's actions that she forwarded me the email with the heading of, "He's an ally!"

I am very lucky to be married to an ally. My husband not only loves me and pushes me to be my best; he is also an ally to me and all women. But Wade was not always an ally. He was never a male chauvinist, or a bad guy. He was just unaware. It took me pointing out the microaggressions for him to see how they affect women. Now he will point them out to the men around him and influence change in the circles he runs in. Most importantly, he does this for more than just his wife. Of course, he wants to protect me from hurtful bias, but more than that, he wants to see other man realize the gender bias they have and how it affects the women around them.

Once, when Wade and I headed out to dinner with a group of our male and female friends. We had decided to split up into two cars with women riding in one and men in another. The men were discussing who would drive when one guy said, "I don't mind riding bitch." Sound familiar? Wade was quick to point out that what he said was a microaggression and aimed at women because traditionally women rode in the passenger seat while men drove.

That turned into a funny interaction between the guys. Our friend tried to explain how he meant that he didn't mind riding in the passenger seat where his female dog rode. While that might not have been a groundbreaking, policy-changing interaction, it was heard and received by Wade's male buddies because it came from a male they respected.

Men can sometimes be more than allies. Some men can be mentors. Male mentors are hard to find. Not because they are not out there or unwilling, but because it's often hard to build that relationship. There is always the concern that when establishing a strictly platonic relationship with someone of the opposite sex things will be misinterpreted. There are also other differences that play a role when finding male mentors.

While most of us like to cut loose and get a little wild, at times we are inclined to hide that part of us until we are with someone we can trust. Ladies, let me make this clear: The person you can trust is your significant other—not your colleagues. Men can be "one of the guys" when they go out drinking, and more often than not, no one notices. If a woman tries to loosen up and goes out drinking with the boys, however, she is putting herself in what is often thought of as a "troublesome spot."

> Getting sloppy drunk isn't a good career move for anyone, man or woman.

Before we go too far down this road, let me stop and say that I rarely drink in professional situations. I often hold a cranberry Sprite cocktail, mainly to avoid being asked why I'm not drinking. I never understood why not drinking is such a big deal, but for whatever reason, it seems to shock people. I personally don't drink often because most times I don't like the taste, and also because I've seen more than a few of my colleagues cross boundaries when they have had one too many. Getting sloppy drunk isn't a good career move for anyone, man or woman. I've seen men wind up in human resources as a consequence of hitting on a female employee after a night of drinking at a company event or socializing after work. I've even seen a woman get fired because she got drunk and started gossiping about her boss. So, I am very careful when it comes to drinking around colleagues.

I am not advocating this policy for every woman. I believe that women have just as much of a right to drink or not drink without fear as a man. Not drinking in professional situations is a personal choice that has served me well in my life. What I am advocating for is being in control of your person, your words, and your professional image.

MEETING WITH THE MEN

Not only do I rarely drink in professional situations, but for years in business, I operated by marriage rules. That meant that I never rode alone in a car with a man, I never had lunch with a man alone, and I never even flew on the same flight with male co-workers.

That can get very tricky. Why do I put those rules on myself? I do so because I value my marriage. I have a healthy marriage, but not a stupid marriage. My marriage is extremely important to me. I have seen marriages fall apart because someone got too close to a co-worker and had an affair. So, I chose to take extreme measures to protect myself from temptation. While not everyone will feel the need to be as protective as I was early in our marriage, the nugget is to ensure that whatever you do, you do in a way that would make you proud if someone posted it on Instagram—or in my case, if Nana saw it on the front page of tomorrow morning's newspaper.

I have loosened up some of those rules. These days, I am not as concerned about having lunch with a male counterpart alone. I let my husband or assistant know where and with whom I am having lunch, and I make it a point to let the male counterpart hear me tell them. I will take the same flight, but not sit next to a male counterpart. In all honesty, I don't sit next to a female co-worker either. I believe a little space is good before a work trip.

It's when joining the boys' club for social and business networking that things can get tricky. That happened once during an out-of-town trip to visit a vendor for demo day at their company headquarters. A demo day is when a company will demonstrate what their product can do. A group of us were picked up at the airport, and, as usual, I was the only woman. During the van ride, one of the men loudly whispered, "So, does it mean we can't go to the strip club because she's here?"

I leaned in and told him, "You can go wherever you want. Just drop me off at the hotel first." Do I have anything against strippers? No, but I'm not going to put myself in a situation where I'm the only woman among a group of men drinking inside a strip club. I don't see how that's going to advance my career, but can hanging with the guys be helpful? Of course. You can also make an impact on your career by taking the higher "leadership" ground.

During a recent plane ride to Miami, Amy Rickman, the former executive with Pfizer, told me this: "Do not peel off from the outing your boss puts on only because you can't play golf or don't like to bowl. These things are social, and social is where 75 percent or more of the real allegiances are exchanged in business. Women are foolish to opt out when they could learn so much about what is really happening and be a part of it. Never go to the spa when your boss, his boss, and all the men you work with are not also at the spa." That was another piece of good advice she gave me, but it was one I had already learned the hard way for myself a few years earlier.

At one point, I served as the president of a local industry board. The day before our annual board meeting, a group of male colleagues all decided to go golfing together. The next day I heard them discussing some of the decisions they had made on the golf course. Decisions they had made without me, the board president. I have no doubt that it was not done out of malice; these were all men I would consider allies—they just didn't think to invite the only girl to go out golfing. *Would I have even gone if they asked?* Maybe, maybe not. I understand the need to have some girl time, so why should I intrude on their guy time? Yet, they weren't some buddies getting together for a Sunday golf game either. They were men who were traveling for a board meeting with other professionals. And they discussed important board decisions while playing golf—discussions I should have been a part of. After going back and forth in my mind about the issue of guy time versus professionals golfing together, I decided that next time, if I wanted to go out with the guys, I'd ask. Or better yet, I'd simply tell them I was going to be joining them.

So, that's what I did. The next time we had an out-of-town meeting, I sent the group an email. "If you guys get together the day before, let me know." And you know what? They did. We all went out to dinner at a microbrewery, and I got valuable information about deals going on in our industry. (And I didn't drink either.) Now they always invite me. Sometimes I say yes, and other times I don't, but taking that weird and awkward first step of making it known that I wanted to be included was all it took.

I know the boys' club isn't necessarily being sexist when they don't invite me out. More often than not, they just don't think of it. So I have to invite myself. Is it awkward? The first time it is, yes, but it gets better, and it gets easier. And as relationships form and friendships grow, it would be unnatural for an ally or friend or mentor to not include you.

WHEN ASKING GOES WRONG

Back when my company was much smaller, I often went on customer visits alone. One time, after meeting with a quality inspector, I gave him my card and told him that if he ever had any issues with our product to please give me a call. He did call, and he asked me out on a date. I told him, "My husband and I would love to have dinner with you." Suddenly, he didn't want to have dinner with me anymore. If you don't have a husband, a similarly effective response is, "My co-worker and I would love to have dinner with you."

In those types of situations, I try to give an easy out for the other person. Even though I've been married for over twenty years, I understand that people in the dating scene have to put themselves out there, so I never fault them for that. As long as they get the hint the first time, and are not vulgar or rude, I handle the situation firmly but kindly.

Have you ever had a moment like this? Unfortunately, I

have also had some "What the heck are you thinking? Don't touch me" moments as well. Thankfully, those moments are few and far between and often out of the blue.

The moments that can be really hard to deal with are the ones that creep up on you. Meaning, the man's behavior rears its head in little installments, which is even more alarming. When a man in your professional world appears to really believe in you and becomes an advocate, ally, or maybe even a mentor, it's devastating to learn that he is interested in more than just your business savvy.

After being in business for years without a real mentor, I thought I had finally found the mentor I had been looking for. He was knowledgeable in business, had a huge network, and gave me creditably just by introducing me to people. He was always happy to teach me and give me pointers on the industry he had been in for over thirty years. We spent hours talking. I even met his wife and adored her. What first drew me to him was that he reminded me of my grandfather, so I respected him immediately.

One night, he invited my husband and me to attend an industry convention with his company. After a day of listening to speakers, I joined him and his colleagues at a restaurant near my hotel. Then, he made a very obvious pass at me. When my husband went to the restaurant, he helped me put on my coat and said, "If anything happens to you and Wade, I've got next!"

I couldn't believe it! I was crushed but tried to laugh it off because he was drunk, then I quickly got the first cab out of there. I never told Wade what happened because I knew he would have said something. And I was also so shocked that I didn't want to deal with it at the moment.

The good news is, he never crossed the line again. The bad news is, he barely spoke to me after that. That stung. I had become accustomed to calling him for business advice and to get his view on certain matters. I thought he really respected me, but his pass made it clear that he thought of me as an object to be claimed. "I've got next" is a phrase I'd heard people use to claim the next game of pool or basketball. It was not a term I wanted spoken about me.

PALE, MALE, AND STALE

It's easy to become jaded and begin to look at every single male in the business world as being against you. Women have to be aware and careful, but not so much so that we don't see people for who they truly are. Men are not the enemy. I have a few men I would consider strong allies. I don't go and have lunch with those men, but I know they are committed to promoting women in leadership. I can't count the number of emails I have received that started with, "Mr. Smith from the State Chamber recommended I speak with you about a position on this board," or "Mr. Smith asked that we reach out to you to get a quote for this article."

One of my favorite male allies is a 70-year-old economic developer by the name of Barry Sellers. Even though Barry is an older white male, he coined the phrase "Pale, Male, and Stale," which he used when referring to the predominantly old white men who are leaders in our community. He would say, "This board is pale, male, and stale, Gina. We've got to get some new blood in there."

There was also Randy Zook, head of my state's chamber of commerce. We have never "hung out" at a non-business or social event, Randy has never met my kids, and I only know his wife from fundraising dinners, but he was quick to recognize my business talent and has invited me to sit at his table many times in many ways. His invite has put me in front of senators, congressmen, and Fortune 500 CEOs that I would have had to otherwise beat down doors to meet, never mind have a conversation of substance with. By introducing me to others, Randy has given me credibility by merely introducing me to others as someone they should know.

> The same way we don't want to be stereotyped, we shouldn't be so quick to stereotype others.

Having male allies is vital. I see so many women bash old white men, but we all know it's the old white men who still have the power, so why would we make them our enemies? For every old white man who calls you sweetheart and is afraid the women and minorities are coming for their power, there are five who genuinely care about promoting women and minorities because they know it is good business. The same way we don't want to be stereotyped, we shouldn't be so quick to stereotype others.

THE LAST WORD

I sat on the board of a local nonprofit homeless shelter that had predominantly male board members. That board was made up of high-level professionals and ran very much like a for-profit corporation. We didn't plan fancy fundraising galas that ended up in the high society section of the newspaper or have an on-staff fundraising professional. We didn't come together and get emotional over the cause of the shelter. Our board meetings were very much down to business.

During one meeting, it was the board's job to determine where a large amount of money was to be allocated. It was clear that one of my fellow board members and I were on opposite sides of the debate about how to use the funds. He and I went back and forth for about five minutes, making point and counter-point about our views on where the funds should go. At one point during the discussion, he looked at the board chairman and said, "Mister Chairman, I have one more statement, and I'd like to have the last word on the matter."

I was stunned. *What? You want the last word? Who do you think you are?* Of course, I did not let the discussion end with his "last word." In that case, I just ignored his request to have the last word, and said, "Mister Chairman, I have more to say." And I continued to make my point. What I found most interesting about his statement was that I have never heard a woman make a statement like that in a boardroom situation. That man believed with everything in him that he commanded enough power to shut down

15 other board members, namely me. He wasn't angry, he wasn't elevated; he didn't even say it in a forceful tone. He was calm and confident. And he truly believed he held the power to have the last word in this conversation.

This is one of those moments where you have a choice: You can get angry, or you can learn. I chose to learn from him. If he could do it, why couldn't I? The very next week, in a meeting with my local chamber, I said the same exact statement in an attempt to move on in respect to everyone's time, and it actually worked. I don't know if the people in the room were not that passionate about what they were arguing about, or if it shocked everyone into silence, but we moved on and ended the meeting on time. I didn't raise my voice or have any emotion behind my statement. It was very likely, however, that once I left that meeting, I was called a bitch (although I doubt anyone thought twice about it when the board member did it to me first), but I didn't care. I was out the door and on my way to enjoy my afternoon.

By watching boardroom bullies, we can learn how to handle them, but we can also learn how to use their tactics to our advantage. If a man can have the guts to say, "I want this to be the last word," so can we!

REFLECTION TIME

As powerful women, we have an opportunity to bridge the gap between our male counterparts. Don't contribute to widening the gap. Instead, look for those allies that are ready to not only learn from you but mentor you. There is more we can learn together than apart when we stop looking for reasons we are different and instead look for ways we can help each other reach the top.

1. What are some of the lessons that you have learned from a male "ally"?

2. As professionals and leaders, we need to empower each other more and be in competition with each other less. What are you doing to be an ally to your fellow professionals?

CHAPTER 4

FINDING YOUR TRIBE

Did you have girls growing up that just treated you like you were less than?

The same way that not all men are out to get us, not all women are here to help us. Evil women do exist! And this is the part of the book where I want to discuss genuinely hateful women.

We've all known the evil, Cruella DeVille-like boss and the "The Plastics" from *Mean Girls*. They are out there. These are the women who will undercut, belittle, lie, gossip, and play games to get ahead. Being a horrible person is not tied to your gender, but yes, these are real bitches in the "hateful female dog" sense of the word. I honestly can't think of a better word to call them. I wish there were one.

The real truth is, this behavior often stems from a lack of self-confidence—those women are not comfortable in their own skin. If they were, they would be happy and wouldn't have a problem with other people's success. Don't be like that and, when at all possible, don't associate with people like that. Find your happiness and look for the good in yourself and others. It's a cliché, but it's true: "Like breed likes," and if you hang out with reprehensible people, guess what...

You can use the tips provided in this book to combat hurtful women, just like their male counterparts. The real hope is that they can see that you are not the enemy and can learn to love themselves. But you are not in control of their self-perception. If they can't see their own worth, then you have to excuse yourself from them until they see both their own worth and yours.

* * *

One reason I should have never let my hair down for the auditor was that I had no reason to fear an audit. I had worked hard to ensure that we had an excellent quality system in place. My employees had worked hard to follow that system. As a matter of fact, the following year, my company managed a perfect score on our audit, with the help of a new auditor, of course. However, simply receiving a perfect score raised suspicion among some of my female colleagues.

A few years after the hair incident, I hired Gemma, an outside consultant, to perform internal quality audits of my company. She and I happened to be two of the very few women in the field at that time in the industry As part of the audit prep process, I showed Gemma our company's past audit results, including the perfect score from the year before.

As we were preparing to head out to lunch, she stepped out to make a phone call. As I exited the building, I overheard her telling one of her co-workers that I must have slept with the auditor to get a perfect score. Once she saw I was standing right there, she hung up and apologized.

"Oh, it's no big deal," I initially told her. But the more I thought about it, the more I realized it was a big deal. "You and I are part of the few females in this field," I said. "I don't need that type of rumor being started."

The worst part was that she was doing the same thing as the male auditor who insinuated that I was the company rep because I was young and female. She assumed that I couldn't receive a perfect score on my own merit. And she was repeating it to others. Even if she said it in a manner that seemed like a harmless joke, jokes like that aren't harmless. The more time I had to think about the incident, the part that bothered me the most was that it was coming from another woman who knew what it was like to be the minority in her field.

WORK WITH (NOT AGAINST) EACH OTHER

Jealousy has existed since the beginning of time. Cain and Abel had a sibling rivalry while cave women were in competition with each other for a man to protect and provide. And for those of us in a male-dominated field, it can feel like there is only room for one woman at the top. but the good news is, that is simply not true. Have you felt like you can be the only successful woman in your space? This is where we bring conflict in on ourselves. We have to remember, the table is big enough for all of us.

Sometimes I wonder if women in predominately male fields enjoy the attention of being the only woman in the group. I don't know if they just like that there is no competition from other women, or if they just don't understand the importance of promoting other woman since there are so few in their industry. There is also the possibility that women are afraid the behavior of another woman will embarrass them. Ladies, you are not the representative of your gender to all others on the earth. Each woman will stand or fall on her own merit.

I'm sure you have examples of when you were undercut by a vicious woman. As women, we have to stop fighting with each other! We have to stop saying things like, "I don't have female friends because they are full of drama." We have to stop gossiping, and we have to stop comparing ourselves to each other. When we find ourselves around a woman or group of women who are backbiting gossips and insecure, we have to remove ourselves. We must take great care not to allow that type of woman to poison us or infect our attitudes.

Seek out and cultivate working relationships with like-minded women who can help you see your own blind spots. Work to build trust with them and look for ways to build them up too. The way to combat the tokenism mentality is to work together to make room for more of us at the top together!

PEOPLE AREN'T ALWAYS
WHO THEY SEEM

In the early days of my career, there was a group of women who volunteered in the nonprofit world who mesmerized me. Those ladies were in all the high-society magazines, carried Prada bags, and ate lunch at members-only clubs. For most of them, volunteering was their full-time job—and I was delighted they had taken an interest in me, a full-time working girl. At that point in my life, the only members-only club I had ever eaten lunch at was Sam's Club. (And they had a great $1.00 hot dog!)

One day during a fundraising committee meeting, it was clear that one of the women, Grace, had been singled out by the group for disapprobation. Every idea Grace had was shot down immediately. At one time during the meeting, I merely repeated Grace's idea and the group loved it, even though they had just shut her down for the same idea.

Once the meeting was over, I asked Grace if she was coming to lunch with us. At that exact moment, my phone buzzed in my hand. I'd received a text from someone else in the group that said, "Not Her." My heart sank. What I had perceived was true. Grace had been singled out by the mean girls. At lunch, they proceeded to talk about how she was fake and only involved with the nonprofit to grow business for herself.

I knew from personal experience and conversations with Grace, however, that was not the case, as I *personally* knew she had a deep connection with the mission of that nonprofit. And I made it a point to mention that connection to the other ladies at our lunch and how I knew the negatives they were saying about her to be absolutely incorrect—but my remonstrances fell on deaf ears.

After lunch that day, I knew that I had a decision to make. I had to either stay in the high-society group and bite my tongue, or I had to remove myself and risk being on the outside. Removing yourself is never easy. I don't care who you are or what stage of life you are in, but it must be done in order to preserve your emotional energy to fulfill your goals in life. You don't have time to reach your goals and deal with backbiting at the same time. That sort of toxic femininity is exhausting, and with all of the mountains you have to climb in your life, it weighs you down.

In the end, I opted to walk away from that group, and to this day don't regret it, not even an ounce. Right is RIGHT!

Of course, you can't always just remove yourself from work, because that can create complicated resume gaps that might affect future employment or business opportunities. What you can do, though, is remove yourself from the negativity at work.

I hate gossip. Hate it! One surefire way that I have found effective is to let the gossips in the group know that you hate gossip. I tell people right up front, "Don't talk about other people to me because I'll tell them what you said." It's amazing how that statement alone will eliminate so much drama in your life. Everyone wants to know the gossip, but no one wants to get caught spreading; thus, they simply quit gossiping to you.

I also tell people, "It's none of my business what goes on in someone else's life, and on top of that, it's none of my business what others think of me." That's exactly what I told the women in the nonprofit group. And I quit attending lunches after the committee meetings. I limited my time with that group of women to just what was necessary—I restricted my involvement to group business and cut out the socialization after meetings.

Did I worry that I had become the center of their gossip and hatefulness? Of course, I did, but every time it crossed my mind, I purposely made myself think of ways to make money. I literally put my mind on my money! And soon enough, I didn't think about, or miss, being a part of that group. I also stopped following those women on social media.

I once came across a meme that said to remove everything that doesn't make you feel good from your social media feeds. That's what I did in my real life as well. I had lived a great life before those women came into it, and I have lived an even better life after them. Here's a great quote from one of my heroes:

> *"Great minds discuss ideas; average minds discuss events; small minds discuss people."*
>
> —ELEANOR ROOSEVELT

THERE ARE GOOD ONES OUT THERE

Imagine if you will, you connect with the bestselling author of a book who brands herself on empowering women, and she actually follows through on that promise.

That was my experience with Heather Monahan, author

of *Confidence Creator.* I downloaded her book on Audible. It's a great book that I highly recommend. One day, out of the blue, I tagged her in an Instagram post, and she responded with a comment. I was shocked! I was even more shocked when she actually called me the next day and freely gave me advice on how to get my own book published.

She's one of the good ones. And guess what? There are many more good ones out there. In my younger years, I had a hard time making female friends. The women I was around were busy backstabbing and gossiping, which means they were jealous of my accomplishment, and further, they were likely talking about me when I was not present. As much as I wanted to be in a friend circle, I would always excuse myself when that stuff started. Eventually, I found a few real friends, and I still love them to this day.

As I have grown into who I am in life and in business, I have surrounded myself with some truly amazing women— *like-minded women.* The Bible says in Proverbs that iron sharpens iron. That was very much by choice. I was intentional about connecting with inspirational women. The ones who are driven and kind. The ones who clap loudly for each other when we succeed and comfort each other when we have setbacks. The hardest thing about finding fellow female go-getter friends is putting ourselves out there.

Where do you even find highly achieving, ambitious women? Sometimes we get lucky and find them in the workplace, or one might happen to be a fellow school mom, but honestly, I have found that to be rare. Not that the other moms at your child's school are not ambitious, driven, and kind, but they are busy. Just like you. And saying, "Hey, let's grab lunch" in the car pool line doesn't seem to work when you are signing field trip permission slips that your child just remembered as he gets out of the car.

What if I don't know women like this? you may ask.

Find your tribe. I have participated in a few different leadership programs on both the state and national level. I highly recommend these types of programs for finding a network of leaders and people who make things happen. I have made great female friends through my nonprofit work. Check with your local and state chambers of commerce to see if they have a leadership program.

This is also where I met a group of women who I consider part of my business tribe. These women are positive. They will speak highly of me when I'm not around and will straighten my crown in private when I need it. I, of course, do the same for them. For the most part, we all work in different fields, yet we all face the same challenges. We've all experienced hateful jealousy from people we thought were friends as we gained success. We can be real with each other. They are my safe place to unload my woes as a woman in business. Having a passion about the same cause can bring people together, but you must be willing to put yourself out there.

This works both ways as well. I received an email from a woman named Katherine after she read an article about me in a local business magazine. She said she connected with the way I was honest about my life. After that initial email, we became close friends and I still keep in touch. We have become sounding boards for each other when it comes to life and business decisions. You want to be the person who you needed when you were new to a group or looking to connect with others.

* * *

When I married Wade, he was in the military. That meant we moved around a lot and frequently relocated to a base where I didn't know anybody. When we moved

> You want to be the person who you needed when you were new to a group or looking to connect with others.

to Eglin Air Force Base in Fort Walton Beach, Florida, I remember attending a spouses' meeting where not one single person took the time to introduce themselves to me. I sat on the side of the room all by myself. It was miserable. Eventually, I walked over to two women who were chatting and said, "No one is talking to me. Do you guys mind if I chat with you?" They were warm and welcoming. They actually apologized for being so caught up in their current friend circle that they didn't notice the new girl.

I decided that day that I would always at least make an attempt to befriend new people in any situation that I could. I can't tell you how many times I've said, "I'd like to get to know you. Can we do lunch or coffee one day?" There have been some lunches that have led to great friendships, and some that ended with a good meal.

I have a saying: "My life is an open door, but not everyone gets invited to the dinner table." Meaning, I love to meet with, encourage, and be encouraged by other women.

However, I am cautious of who I let into my inner circle, or in my tribe, if you will. Watch out for people who always have something negative to say. Nope, not my tribe! Nice lunch!

One red flag for me is a woman who talks about other people. Whether it's telling someone's business or talking about how the person at the table next to us is dressed. That's a huge no-no, and it tells you that the person can't be trusted to bring positive vibes into your life. Let that end with a good lunch.

If a woman talks more about her possessions than her passions? Nice lunch. Be firm in your convictions about who you let into your life. People with positive energy can lift you up and energize you. People with negative energy will emotionally exhaust and drain you.

> Be firm in your convictions about who you let into your life.

If you put yourself out there, you will find your tribe. I can promise you that there are positive women just waiting to form a tribe with you. You just have to look for them—they have to know you're "there."

HOLD YOURSELF TO THE SAME STANDARD

What standard are you holding yourself to? Sometimes when we find that we have a lack of true and honest friends, we need to do some self-evaluation. Do you know why I hate gossip so much? Because I used to be one.

In middle school, I would talk about everyone's business. It was an honest comment from a friend that made me change my ways. I had found out that my best friend had secretly been dating a teacher's son. I was so hurt that she didn't tell me. When I asked her why, she said it was because she didn't want the whole school to know. Ouch! Talk about a wake-up call. I can still picture that conversation in my mind. I can still feel the sting of those words like a strong slap across the face, and the feeling in my gut that she was right. All these years later, I am still grateful for that conversation. It has made me a better person. Not a perfect person, by any means, but I can honestly say that I am a better friend thanks to learning that lesson as a young woman.

> It's always better to be a good listener than a good talker.

How do you become a good tribe member? Start by being someone who listens. It's always better to be a good listener than a good talker. My mother always said, "The reason God gave you two ears and one month is so you can listen twice as much as you speak."

This is especially true in mixed company because you NEVER want to say anything bad about someone else in public, because you never know who's listening. I can't tell you how many times I've heard people say something rude or hateful about someone, and the person they were speaking to happened to be a friend of the person they had just insulted. That's the quickest way to get on people's wrong side and ruin your reputation, and maybe even your business. If you don't want to find yourself on the other side of conflict, don't say something about someone else in public you wouldn't want them to say about you.

I have a general rule: I always say something nice about everyone. Even if I can't stand that person, I find at least one good thing to say about them if their name comes up in conversation. Even if it's just, "She's very photogenic!" That has served me well over the years, and once it even saved a friendship.

A negative person who enjoyed starting trouble told a friend of mine that I had said something negative about her. My friend thought about it for a second and said, "I don't believe that. Even if Gina hated me, she would say I was photogenic!"

If I'm being honest, I had to learn that one the hard way. I used to honestly believe that with my success came the right to say whatever I wanted. I thought that by calling people out or saying any negative thing that came to my mind, it was just me telling it like it is. And that's what a no-nonsense successful woman does, right? Well, it's only what the woman who wants to end up all alone with a broken network does.

Long story short: If you want to grow a network of

> If you want to grow a network of positive and powerful women, become a positive and powerful woman.

positive and powerful women, become a positive and powerful woman.

WORDS OF WISDOM

Amy Rickman told me that in all her 26 years with Pfizer, she never had a female mentor. This was because there were no females in higher positions at Pfizer yet. She looked up to her male bosses who were very supportive of her even back in the early 1980s. Her story is unusual, but it appears that Pfizer Inc. got it right over 40 years ago when they hired women to join their sales force. Amy told me that she was one of maybe five women in a team of over 200 men, which is why she goes out of her way to mentor women. She even shared with me some of the advice that she passes along to her mentees:

- Eighty percent of success is showing up. If we never show up, we can't get lucky.

- Success is a marathon, not a sprint.

- The unfortunate and inept are one in the same.

- If you are not smart enough to know who to kiss up to, you might not be smart enough for the job.

- People do not do stupid things, they make bad decisions.

- You make your decisions first, and then they make you.

- Communication is 55 percent nonverbal, 38 percent tone of voice, and 7 percent what is spoken. That is why the way you dress (including whether or not you have shined shoes, a good haircut, and clean fingernails) and how often you smile are so important. Your appearance is like a billboard advertising about YOU. It's about being polished and friendly, not about being pretty. It's about your personal ethos. If you are slovenly in appearance, you're probably going to be lax in your work ethic and quality of production, keeping commitments, and other areas in life. You think that's not fair, that I'm prejudging or profiling? I am. So do you. Example: Have you ever walked into a public restroom and then turned right around to find another cleaner, more hygienic one? Same thing, it's just I'm doing it with people.

- *No* doesn't always mean "no"—many times it just means not right now, which is why Amy taught her team to call on offices at least eight times before getting discouraged.

- NEVER QUIT OVER A BAD DAY!

Amy tells the story of mentoring a woman who wrote on her resume that "jogging" was her hobby. Lots of people like to jog, so it didn't really stand out. What the woman didn't articulate was that she had run in the London, Boston, and New York marathons and was training for her fourth. The information on her resume was actually misleading, so they changed her hobby from "jogging" to "distance runner," which helped her stand out. That is typical of how a woman will downplay her achievements. It's important for women to take pride in their accomplishments. Put your best foot forward and make sure they see the designer shoe.

Because, much like Amy, I had so few female mentors when I started out, I have resolved to go out of my way to mentor so many women today. It's such a wonderful feeling to see someone you have mentored achieve success and personal fulfillment. Be the person you needed to help you back when you started out.

MENTORS NEEDED!

With only 14 percent of C-level positions being held by females, and yet 52 percent of the workforce is female, there is a massive gap in female mentorship for women seeking a C-suite mentor. And there is even a more significant gap for female CEOs looking for mentors with only 5 percent of CEOs being women. Odds are much more in favor of men finding a male mentor.

You don't need to have it all to become a mentor. You just need to come from a certain field or have a specific skill set. Over the years, I've had mentors who were mothers, business owners, and PhDs. A good mentor requires good judgment and someone who is willing to tell the hard truths. It's also important that your mentor is someone who you can trust, and someone who has your best interest at heart. You want your talks to remain quiet. As we say in the South, make sure that your mentor has open ears and a closed mouth.

At the beginning of my career, I would try to ask a woman in leadership to be my mentor. My ask was often met with statements such as, "I should be asking you to mentor me." While this was flattering, it was not helpful at all. I was lucky to have a grandfather who was an international businessman for a large textile company. He served as a great business mentor for me, but for all the great business advice he gave me, he could never tell me what it was like to be a woman in business.

That's where I can become most helpful to others, and even though every person is different and requires a different type of guidance, there is a theme to much of the advice I give, and it comes from what my grandfather once told me: "Your business should be about your customers, not you."

> Your business should be about your customers, not you.

At the beginning of my career, he told me to hire a CPA and a lawyer, but to always remember that business is about the customers. That advice can sting because many people start their own businesses for freedom. Well, most men go into business for freedom from a boss, and most women go into business out of necessity. If your business is all about you, soon you won't have a business.

YOUR CUSTOMER IS YOUR BRAND

Take some time to scroll through your business social media accounts. Are the photos of you, or are they of your product and clients?

Brag about your products and clients. Let your clients brag about you. That is solid advice no matter what you do for a living. It doesn't matter if you are in a service-based industry or a product industry. It doesn't matter if you are the owner of a business or just starting your career.

People are emotional creatures. Our buying habits are driven by our emotions. That is important to remember, because people will spend money on things that make them feel good, including businesses that make them feel special.

If you post a photo of your customer on your social media and say how honored you are to have them as a customer, not only will they return, they will share the post and tell friends about your service or product. That is earned media and free marketing! That is why all the marketing gurus ask people on Instagram to be brand ambassadors. Successful companies know that people are emotional beings who want to be like others they admire. People want to see themselves as valuable. They want fame—even if that fame lasts but ten seconds on social media because they bought your product or service. All because you put the spotlight on *them*. All because you said *they* were special. ALL BECAUSE YOU MADE THEM FEEL GOOD. A smile costs nothing for you to give away.

I cannot tell you how many referrals I have given to businesses because of connections on social media. Either the company or I will post about using their products or services. Often, when one of my connections needs or wants that particular service, they reach out to me and ask about the post, or they simply call the business and say that I referred them. I once shared a post about getting a lash lift that the business posted on their social media sites. The businesswoman called me to say she had gotten three new clients that very day, all of whom where connections of mine on social media who mentioned my post when booking their appointments.

Trust me when I say this: *You are not your brand.* Unless you are already famous and selling sheets with your name on them, you are not the brand. And even if you are famous and selling sheets with your name on them, online customer reviews can take you down in a minute. Again, *it's the customers who hold the power.* So make them feel special, and they, in turn, will give you free marketing—marketing that comes with a built-in trust from their connections because their connections trust them to have good taste and good values. You can't buy that kind of marketing for any amount of money! Businesses offer discounts if people refer others to them because they know what works. By marketing your customers, you are getting the referrals without having to offer the discount.

> Make your customers your brand.

Make your customers your brand. It just makes good business sense.

LISTEN TO YOUR CLIENTS

When I receive requests to mentor people, they have often reached a point where their business or career has stalled. If that's the case and they ask me for help, my first question is, "What are your customers saying?"

I don't care if you're in marketing, real estate, IT, manufacturing, or product innovations, you have to listen to your clients. Ask them for honest feedback, even if it's painful for you to hear—especially if it's painful for you to hear. The following is a story of two separate business owners and why I quit using their services. It was their reaction afterward that made the difference in which one went on to be successful and which one eventually went out of business.

The first was Payton, an esthetician I went to for facials. For about eight months, I had a regular schedule of getting a facial every other week. Twice, Payton smelled like cigarettes, and I asked her on each occasion if she smoked, and each time she told me that she didn't.

There are two things I can't stand—the smell of cigarettes and a liar. If you are rubbing your hands on my face, I can certainly tell if you smoke or not. So I stopped using Payton's services. I didn't give her an explanation; I just quit making appointments.

About four months later, I received a call from her, asking why I had not been in for the past several months. She was very professional, kind, and sincere, so I responded in the same way and made sure to tell her the truth. I knew that telling her the truth with the same kindness and respect she displayed when inquiring of my absence would help her in her career. She apologized, sent me a gift certificate for a free facial, and said that if I gave her another opportunity, it would never happen again.

Since that conversation, I mentored Payton as her business grew. A few years later, Payton thanked me for being honest with her. She stated that our interaction was an eye-opening experience. Because she sincerely asked why

I didn't use her services anymore, I was able to point out a blind spot that she would never have thought of on her own. It had not occurred to her that she smelled like cigarettes and that the smell could be offensive to some of her clients. She now owns her own spa, and she briefs all new staff on our interaction. And because she listened to her clients, she turned an unhappy customer into a lifelong mentor.

The second example also occurred in the beauty industry. I hired Alexus as a makeup artist for event styling. I would visit her about four or five times a month over a year and a half. I liked her as a stylist, but she had a bad habit of gossiping about her clients. She would use her clients' actual names and say things like, "Mary Smith's daughter is in a cult," or the one that really got me: "Samantha Beal said that Tina Jones's husband was a real jerk." Full names, people! Not even "I have a client who told me…" Full. Names.

On more than on occasion, I made statements about how gossip made me feel uncomfortable and how I firmly believed that if she was going to talk about others to me, then she would have no problem talking about me to others. While the actual service was excellent, Alexus simply could not stop herself from gossiping, even after I repeatedly told her I didn't like it. As a result, I stopped using Alexus's services.

A few months later, I received a social media message from Alexus. She felt there was negative energy between the two of us, and she didn't know why. Alexus then suggested that we meet for a drink and chat. She did not ask for any feedback. She didn't even acknowledge that I was no longer using her business services. In fact, Alexus didn't act like a business owner at all. The nature of the conversation prevented Alexus from getting any valuable feedback and cost her a customer.

It actually cost her a few customers because when asked who I recommended for that service, I no longer referred people to Alexus. Eventually, some of her other customers left explicitly because of the gossiping in the salon. She lost money because she made the business about herself and the information she knew, not about the customers. Even more telling was the fact that Alexus's ego prevented her from asking for feedback that could have changed the only negative thing she had going on in her business. Over the following years, her business slowly died.

You must stay vigilant when appealing to your customers' wants and needs. The idea of branding yourself over your customers and clients will eventually put you out of business.

Never forget: *People support people who support them.*

REFLECTION TIME

It's easy to feel as if your success is dependent on someone else losing so you can reach your goals. If you work and compose yourself with the utmost integrity, you can lead others and create success without leaving a trail of bodies in your wake.

1. What are three things you can start doing today to mentor or support other leaders in business?

2. What are three ways you can get honest feedback from your clients?

CHAPTER 5

FINDING THE BALANCE

Are you trying to do everything? Whenever I speak to a group of women, the number one question I'm asked is, "How do you do it all?" followed by, "How do you find that work-life balance?" I've gotten those questions so many times that I probably should have titled this book *How to Do It All!* It would have been a best seller for sure!

I firmly believe this is a uniquely feminine question. No one has ever asked my husband how he balances being a business owner and a father, but as women, we have this almost inherent guilt that keeps us thinking we have to do everything. We have to be a caring mother who puts her children first, which means we bake goodies for the class, attend PTA meetings, drive our kids to every sport and activity known to humankind, dress them correctly, and help with homework. At work, we have to be on time, prepared, professional, and stylish while simultaneously networking, balancing the books, leading projects, keeping our cool, and empowering others. Then, of course, after working all day, we come home to cook a healthy, Instagramable dinner and still leave time to clean the house, hit the gym, and have a lovely bath before our bedtime routine. Oh, and if you're married, you have to be able to turn into a sexy vixen after the kids are in bed. Somewhere in between being a successful career woman, a perfect mom, a gourmet chef, and a hot wife, you have to work out, have a girls' night out, get a clay facial, and get at least eight hours of sleep each night.

This is instilled at a young age. I didn't realize how young until I was invited to speak to a group of business students at a private university. After speaking, I was approached by a 20-year-old woman named Tamara who asked if I thought she should stay in business school. Tamara had taken a summer job in the quality department at a manufacturing company near her hometown. She absolutely loved that job, and she loved everything she was learning in business school. She stated she enjoyed it so much that it worried her because she hoped to one day be a wife and a mother.

For a moment, I just stared at this sweet petite girl in shock. *If she loved her job and loved business, then why would she quit just because she wants to get married and have children?* Then it hit me with a force equal to every woman in the world yelling at the same time: SHE THINKS SHE HAS TO BE PERFECT!

I looked deep into her blue eyes. "You can do both," I said. "You just have to give up the idea that you have to be perfect."

Her body stiffened, and she shook her head as her eyes filled with tears. She didn't say another word. It was clear that she did not realize it was an option.

It felt so good to pass along important advice to a twentysomething and convince her that she didn't have to fit an unrealistic mold, something I didn't personally learn until I was in my thirties.

Repeat after me. You don't have to be perfect!

SO HOW DO I BALANCE IT ALL?

I DON'T! I QUIT!

First, and most importantly, when I realized the degree to which unrealistic expectations for myself were hindering my true happiness, I quit having unrealistic expectations of myself and my family.

For me, that started with the way my sons dressed. Most of my morning energy was put into fighting with them so they didn't look homeless when they left the house. My older son was a skateboarder. That meant his shoes were always torn up. And of course, he did not want to wear the nice shoes I bought him because he could not skate in them. Once I took a little time and reflected on why I wanted them to dress like GAP models, I realized it was because I thought their appearance was a direct reflection on my mothering skills.

After that self-awareness moment, I realized my sons were loved, well cared for, well fed, and happy. I was only creating more work for myself by fighting over an image they cared nothing about—an image that had nothing to do with their personalities or interests, but one I had conjured up in my head as to what the sons of a perfect mother dressed like. It had no basis in reality.

So I started letting them wear whatever they wanted. I only asked that they dressed nicely on Sundays, Mother's Day, and my birthday. And guess what? I didn't die of shame. Child Protective Services did not come to take my children. And we were all happier with our newfound freedom from that awful thing called image.

I quit thinking my house had to be perfect. I began to joke about how I left my house messy because "I don't want the other moms to feel they have to live up to my standards. So, in reality, my messy house is a service to others." It started as a joke, but quickly opened the door to many conversations about the unrealistic expectations we put on ourselves.

> I don't want the other moms to feel they have to live up to my standards.

I quit cooking dinner every night. The Crock-Pot became my best friend. I discovered that fixing meals that were new and adventurous was not something I enjoyed, and neither did my family. And guess what? Kids love to eat cereal for dinner! And no one died of malnutrition.

I quit being the mom who attends everything. I told my sons they had to pick one activity at a time. No more would we be driving from soccer practice to karate. One activity at a time! They loved that because that meant they got to choose what was important to them.

I applied the "one activity at a time" rule to myself. I quit volunteering for every fundraiser and committee in my church and community.

I quit doing things that other people could do for themselves. I realized that my sons could do their own laundry. They were so small they would have to jump up and lean into the washer to transfer their clothes from the washer to dryer, but they did it. That stopped them from putting clean clothes in the hamper. Once they realized they were adding more work for themselves, it was amazing to see the difference in how many clothes actually made it into their drawers, and how little laundry they had.

They cleaned their own rooms and the bathroom. And if it wasn't perfect, I didn't redo it. I pointed it out, and they did it. I didn't expect perfection. Plus, I paid a high school student $30 every other week to do a once-over of the house—vacuum, dust, and clean my room. I told my sons that if they wanted her to clean their rooms, they would have to pay her.

Was my house perfect? Not by a long shot, but I realized that having a perfect home was not a priority for me. *Being sane and happy was my priority.*

I found out that my husband was happy to take the boys to school in the mornings. Between that and not fighting about what my kids wore, I had enough time to start working out in the mornings. Removing the expectation of perfection actually gave me time back!

At work, I took the time to teach my staff tasks that I could delegate to them. And, as my company grew, I hired an assistant. That was the turning point for me in my workplace. Hiring Amy was one of the smartest and most liberating things I could have done. She handles my calendar, appointments, travel arrangements, and so much more. She indeed is a life saver. I know that not everyone can hire an assistant. Either way, you have to prioritize, and it all comes down to what you personally give yourself permission to quit that will make the difference in your personal life and overall well-being.

Anyone, no matter if you're a stay-at-home mom or the CEO of a fast-growing company, can quit doing things that don't bring value to your life. The biggest step for me was when I quit feeling like I had to control everything. It wasn't easy, and sometimes I still find myself doing things that others can do, but it was the best thing for me.

> Quit doing things that don't bring value to your life.

The need to find balance and do it all comes from our need to control it all—controlling the outcome because we think we can do it better, and controlling our image because of what people would think if our children showed up to school looking crazy.

The more I looked into my motivation to take on too many tasks, I realized it all connected back to my need to control everything. It was difficult, but once I was able to free myself from that need, I found the real key to balance.

So I quit. I quit doing things that others could do for themselves. I quit doing things others could do for me. And I quit trying to be perfect and please everyone. I realized that I was trying to be all things to all people. For my own sanity, I had to quit. And finally, after all of that, I quit caring what others thought about me quitting.

WE INSTINCTIVELY SAY YES

The truth is, trying to do it all will only exhaust you and prevent you from getting ahead, personally and professionally. I have become quite certain that the need to do it all is much more common in the woman's world than it is in a man's world.

As you advance in your career, you may notice that men hold executive positions while women tend to be the doers. We all have heard of the executive who couldn't survive the day without the all-knowing, all-doing (most often female) assistant who runs everything behind the scenes.

> The need to do it all is much more common in the woman's world than it is in a man's world.

Let's use the example of the nonprofit and networking world. When entering a chamber meeting, it's rare to see a man taking tickets at the door. There are many reasons for that. Women tend to be more organized; we tend to ask other women for help, and women typically work in more service industries, which makes us natural at being doers. But more importantly, and most often, women say yes.

Women are notorious for always saying yes. We take on far too many tasks by saying yes to small things that we shouldn't be doing. Why do we do this? Let's see:

- We were raised to be helpful.

- We don't want to seem like a bitch.

- We don't want anyone to think we are above a particular type of work.

- We are people pleasers.

- We want to be perfect.

- We have a fear of missing out (FOMO) .

And of course, we have the above-mentioned need to control.

MY FIRST NO

I distinctly remember when I decided to start saying no. It was when I had become overwhelmed in all areas of my life. My business was growing, my children were active in school, and I volunteered at church, PTA, and at a homeless shelter. Did I mention parenting, housework, and being a wife? In the great buffet line of life, my plate was too full.

I remember having a mini meltdown after traveling to three different states in one week, cooking for and attending a three-hour chili cook-off at my son's school, and working over 40 hours in the office. And then I LMS on Saturday morning when my boys weren't doing their chores fast enough for me because I wanted us to enjoy half a day together doing an Instagram-able family outing.

That's when my husband dared to ask the question that has likely sent many a man to the ER, "What the heck is wrong with you? It's not that big of a deal."

I erupted in a screaming fit.

I had so much on my plate that my head was spinning, and it felt like I couldn't get any support from my family to do something as simple as picking up after themselves.

My husband calmly reminded me that I didn't have to do everything.

I gave him such a blank stare that he thought I went into shock. I was certain he had clearly not noticed that the world only spun on its axis because I kept it moving by doing everything that needed to be done.

But he was right.

For the first time in my life, it dawned on me that I didn't have to do all those things. I needed to start getting rid of the tasks and duties that didn't bring me joy or propel me forward.

Any good executive or entrepreneur will tell you that the key to growing your business is delegation. In my case, as in most women's case, delegation starts with saying no.

The opportunity presented itself just three days after my LMS meltdown.

At the time, I was serving on the board of directors for a local charity nonprofit. That board had a lot of local VIPs on it, and I was amazed that I got to rub elbows with them. When the board president came to me and asked if I would be willing to be the board secretary, which he pointed out would make me part of the executive committee, it was tempting for me to say yes in that instant, only to say no the next day. I thought about it for about 10 seconds, then with all the wisdom of a much wiser, older, and—dare I admit it—possibly more male person, I said no.

I explained that my life had become very busy, and soon I would have to cut something out in order to keep up with my growing family and career. I told him I didn't like to take notes, nor did I have the time to type them up, and while I very much enjoyed my work with the board, if I took the board secretary position, it would make my involvement much less enjoyable due to the extra work. I explained that as things got overwhelming in life, I had learned to cut out the commitments that didn't bring me joy and that speaking prospectively, it was likely I would step off the board when the time came to make my life less stressful because of my family and business obligations that were only increasing, not decreasing. What that meant right then was, because of my love for the organization, I would have to decline.

While that was entirely more information than he needed to know, the president said, "Well, that's disappointing but understandable." Then he immediately went over to the only other female on the board to offer her the job, and she became the secretary.

Guess what? I didn't die. The organization didn't fall apart, and they didn't hate me. Instead, a year and a half later, I was voted vice president of the board and later became the president to help transition the charity through a tough time and into new leadership.

This inspired me to conduct a little experiment of my own. I asked a few men to help with small tasks at a chamber event, taking tickets at the door before our monthly luncheon. And you know what I heard? "No, I can't." You see, I had been asked to take tickets at the door, and when I said no, I asked if they had asked any of my male colleagues. It was no surprise that they had not, so I decided to ask some men in the organization, as well as women, to see what kind of response I would get. The response I received from the men in the organization fell into two categories that went something like this:

- "I can't because that requires me to be here early and I don't have the time."
- "I don't think that will work for me. Have you tried to ask Susie? She's very helpful."

Call me skeptical, but I'm pretty sure we all operate on the same 24-hour-a-day schedule.

I asked both male and female bankers, insurance agents, and people running for the same seat for office. All the men said no—even a male insurance intern said no. The men weren't rude; they were just unapologetic in their noes. On the other hand, almost all the women said yes or at least something along the line of, "I really can't, but if you can't find someone else, I'll do it."

MORE PRACTICE SAYING NO

My next no came at church. I know, right? I surely thought the gates of hell would open to let me in!

When initially I had been asked to speak at a women's conference that my church was holding, I had gladly accepted. Then, when I was asked if I could facilitate the prayer group for the event (a much more significant and more administrative-type role than I could realistically commit to) and said no, not only did I say no, but I said no in front of the whole organizing committee. It felt like my no sucked all the air out of the room. Because I didn't want people to think I thought I was too good for that job, I felt the need to explain myself, so I stated the facts: The event was being held on the Saturday after I was scheduled to return from a large trade show around midnight the morning of the event, and I didn't feel a worn-out and exhausted me would be able to do the job justice. Explanation given, I took a breath and waited for the gates of hell to slam shut on me.

So what happened?

The person in charge of the event was a successful businesswoman about ten years my senior. She looked at me and said, "That makes perfect sense to me. Thank you for being honest."

Again, I didn't die, and nobody hated me, including Jesus. As a matter of fact, I gained the respect of a woman I really looked up to. Most importantly, I didn't say yes and run the risk of a meltdown by stretching myself too thin.

It may sound silly, but another small way I was able to practice saying no occurred at Sam's Club. Yes, Sam's Club. I used to be the woman who took every single sample because I didn't want the workers to feel rejected. Have you ever caught yourself doing that? If so, have you ever thought about how you're adding extra calories and fat to your diet just to avoid hurting someone else's feelings? Stop that!

Saying no is another form of self-care. Don't worry, saying no thoughtfully and politely does not make you a bitch.

I know how easy it is to feel like that. Ladies, we have to stop worrying about being viewed as a bitch. A wise man once told me, people are going to call you one anyway, so you might as well do what you want!

DOING IT ALL (ALL HAIL THE "PEOPLE PLEASER")

When I was speaking at an event for college students, a female student in the audience said to me, "I'm offended. All you talked about was race, felons, and foster care."

I had already given business advice, and her question was the perfect segue for me to talk about why I do what I do. I explained that my passion was to help those who possibly had not had the same opportunities that I had. I explained that I hire people who have had felonies in the past. Then I explained that children who do not get adopted within the state's foster care system before their eighteenth birthday "age out at 4 p.m. on their eighteenth birthday" (that means, *Happy birthday, goodbye, and good luck, adult*), and that more often than not, these castaways/orphans out on the streets on their own become homeless and/or end up in prison. Once I became aware of that, I made it a personal purpose to mentor young people who came out of the foster care system. And because I think diversity is important, I spoke about starting an internship with the local HBCU (historically black college & university) to encourage women of color to go into engineering fields.

I took the time to answer the young lady and encouraged her to continue the conversation as she got up and left the room. After I had spoken with other students and said my goodbyes, I went and found the student and listened to her talk at length. We had what I had hoped was a healing conversation. As a fortysomething woman speaking to a young female in an era when the culture in America feels particularly unaccepting of both her sex and age, I made a conscious choice to simply listen to the young woman. I didn't defend my actions or my statements. I didn't try to make her see it my way. I gave grace to the fact that she was hurt and aiming her anger at the stereotype of what she perceived a 40-year-old woman to be, and not at my actual self.

I think we both learned something that day. We ended the conversation with a hug. If the outcome of our conversation had settled things in my mind, I would have walked away a happy woman—but it did not. I walked away feeling I had failed miserably for offending someone, no matter that it was unintended and that I was honestly trying to inspire the group to affirmatively seek to make a difference in others' lives. I could not get it off my mind and literally obsessed over it for two days. I couldn't sleep. I read every blog I could find about how to be a white ally to people of color, how to speak to the needs of college students, how to be an ally to those previously incarnated—everything I could find about the subjects that offended her. While I am sure there are things worse than being misperceived and misunderstood, I sure couldn't think of any that week.

Then I saw the video of my speech. The student who told me she was offended was seated at the table directly in front. She was in view of the camera the entire time and did not face me once during my speech. In fact, she looked upset from the moment she sat down, long before I had said anything about felons, diversity, or foster care. She rolled her eyes frequently when I spoke. It was clear that she was upset by something before I ever even started speaking and wasn't triggered by any of the subjects I discussed that she told me offended her.

The overall conversation I was able to have with her after was still a teachable moment for us both, but what stood out most to me about the situation was the fact that I was so obsessed with everyone liking me that I was willing to assume that I had done something wrong. I was so hurt over it that I beat myself up for two days. I even thought about canceling the other speaking engagements I had that week because I thought I wasn't good enough. I almost let an 18-year-old college student stop me because I was such a people pleaser. But thank God for the video because it allowed me to see the reality of the situation. More importantly, it snapped me out of my people-pleasing ways.

While I do believe that the young lady has had to deal with issues and microaggressions on levels that I may never understand, I also realized that I, personally, could not solve all the hurt that she had encountered. Nor was it my job to please everyone in the world. Hey, not everyone is going to like you. Period.

My friends tried to tell me about that for years. It connects back to what I wrote about earlier when it came to me apologizing for my success. I really wanted people to like me. I didn't want people to think that I thought I was better than they were. When someone didn't like me, I obsessed over it. I tried to run back conversations in my mind to see where I went wrong. I told myself that I was being self-reflective to better myself, but it was a reoccurring theme in my life. I had enough self-confidence not to let myself be mistreated by others, but I didn't realize that I was mistreating myself.

Today, I follow the 24-hour rule. If I feel that I have offended someone, I ask myself: Is there a better way for me to say what I said? If yes, I write it down and attempt to make amends. If no, I move on. I'm not allowed to think about the situation for more than 24 hours. I can't let it take up mental space, living rent-free in my head. If I find myself fixating thinking about it, I force myself to think about something positive and uplifting instead. It was a challenge at first, but it gets easier every time. It's really about training your mind.

I do my best to help others. But I can't and won't always please everyone. If they don't like it, that's not my concern. I mean, look at Jesus—not everyone liked him, so what chance do I have? I've grown to realize other people's opinions of me are no longer my concern. Once I achieved living that mindset, it was an incredibly liberating thing that gave me emotional freedom as I had never known before!

HARD WORK INCLUDES SELF-CARE

Do you need self-care? Take a look at the top drawer in your dresser. Do all of your panties have holes in them? Is the underwire poking out of your bra?

Ashley, the business manager for one of my companies, recalls the time when she first realized she needed self-care.

"I had been wearing the same contacts for a month, had gone without a haircut, my shoes were four years old, and my cell phone was so old that I couldn't even find chargers for it! And any time my husband would ask for something, I found myself biting his head off. I realized that I wasn't prioritizing my health and maintenance. As women, we try to 'be all that we can be' 24 hours a day, and we can't do it all!"

And I think the army at war metaphor is totally apropos for a career woman trying to do it all so she can have it all and be the end all be all for her husband and kids. Back to Dirty Harry, "we gotta know our limitations."

We have to take care of ourselves *first* so we can take care of others. When you're on an airliner, the attendants in their pre-takeoff instructions always tell you in the event of an emergency to put on *your* oxygen mask first and then your child's, as if you pass out both you and your child are likely to have a bad result. It's not being selfish to make sure you don't pass out—it's being smart! That's why doctors, nurses, and EMTs get the flu vaccine first. Think about it? If they start dropping sick, who will take care of the people flocking the emergency rooms? If you're rescuing a drowning person, you are instructed to take care to approach them from the rear and knock them out if you have to in order to keep them from inadvertently drowning you while you're trying to save them. It makes absolute sense to take care of you so you can take care of all you do.

In the world of trying to be all things to all people, we very easily forget to take care of ourselves, even in the smallest of ways. Today, you always hear women refer to spa treatment or shopping as self-care, but not all self-care needs to cost hundreds of dollars. Why do we even need self-care? I don't recall ever hearing a man say he needed self-care. Why? Because they have hobbies, and more often than not, when they get home, they don't feel the need to clean the house, fix dinner, attend a PTA meeting, and spend quality time with the kids. And even if you are blessed with a husband who does all that, they don't feel the need to be perfect. It's striving to be perfect and do everything that drives women to seek self-care, or more likely, have Saturday morning LMS meltdowns.

Have you ever wanted to check into a hotel and just sleep for a few days? Have you ever returned from a so-called "relaxing" vacation more stressed-out and exhausted than you were before you left? I have spent time on a beautiful beach where I could smell the salt water and watched the waves crash on the pristine shoreline only to feel completely panicked about not being able to relax. My personal favorite is when I return from a spa day only to realize that it wasn't nearly as elegant or romantic as everyone's posts on Instagram made it seem.

So many of us take care of our bodies and our outward appearance, and think we are providing ourselves self-care. I personally hate to have my nails done. I love the way they look and have them done, but I hate the process. I don't want to sit still for 30 minutes and not be able to use my hands. It's not comfortable to sit in a chair with my arms stretched out. I do love a good pedicure, but it's not the unwinding experience of mind, body, and soul that it's made out to be. Having to sit next to a woman talking loudly on her phone about who knows what is not relaxing in the least. That's not self-care to me. It seems more like "social care." I keep my nails nice because it fits more into what society deems that a polished career woman should look like.

Rarely is real self-care the Instagram-able experience we want it to be. Sometimes it's as small as taking the time to refresh our underwear drawer. Self-care must be a way of life for us. The truth is that there is no quick fix for total self-care. Self-care, just like self-love, must come from within. I break it down into three categories: mind, body, and soul.

MIND

Self-care of your mind starts with releasing things you cannot control. As women, we tend to want to control everything. And not being able to do that that drives us insane!

Instead, do things that improve your mental well-being. Spend an evening with your tribe talking over frustrating things. I have spent nights with my friends talking until 2 a.m. and woke up feeling totally revived the next morning. Talking things out helps!

Feed your mind with positive affirmations. I use Twitter and Instagram to follow people who continuously post positive quotes about life and business. I use Audible to listen to books on business and life. If you spend just 20 minutes each day inputting positive affirmations into your mind, you will be shocked at how much more in life you can handle. And if you take affirmative steps to eliminate as much as possible negative mindsets from taking root like weeds in your mental garden, you are that much more ahead of the game.

Spend time with people who energize you and avoid those who drain you. I realize that family and friendships can be draining and some of those relationships are unavoidable. However, you can strengthen your mind. Try adding a positive twist during your conversations and interactions with those more difficult people.

I have a family member who continually focuses on the negatives, whether it's professionally or personally. It's draining, so when speaking with her, I try to say things like, "Oh, changing the subject, I thought it was wonderful how this happened..." Eventually, she'll either transition to a more positive topic, or at least stop bringing up negative things. Of course, if you have someone in genuine need or physical pain, it's quite possible you can uplift them—not all people who need mentoring are unrelated to us.

BODY

I have started consistently working out over the past few years. It started with a neck injury that sent me to physical therapy. After so many sessions, my physical therapist told me that I had come as far as I could with him, and the best thing to keep me out of pain was to strengthen my muscles. Working out not only helped lessen my pain, but I woke up each day with a clear mind. I also began to eat healthier by avoiding sugar and processed foods. That improved my skin and overall health.

Suddenly, I realized that I had more energy and I slept

better, which meant I was more productive and could focus on all the things I needed to get done. That was a game changer. I began to feel better about the way I looked in my clothes. I no longer pulled at my shirts or dresses, trying to cover up areas I was unhappy with. I had confidence in the way I felt and looked. I now relieve stress on the gym floor, rather than carry it around with me for days. Distance runners refer to an endorphin rush—and it's true! Exercise causes the release of body chemicals that make you feel exhilarated, vibrant, and more alive. Try it!

SOUL

I am a strong believer in Jesus Christ. I turn to my faith to renew my soul. Every day I read a chapter in Proverbs from the Bible to gain wisdom, and I spend time praying and meditating to center myself. For millions, faith is the staple of their lives. Whatever your faith (a spiritual being, the earth, or science), spending time renewing your soul is the best self-care there is.

Sometimes just lying in the grass and listening to the wind can bring peace to your soul. Practice mindful (deliberate) breathing. Focus on each breath as it comes in through your nose and out through your mouth. Spend time with friends who uplift you and make you laugh. Oh, one more thing: ***Laughter is good for the soul.***

When life begins to stress me out to the point that I can't sleep, I remember the familiar lyrics to a song by Irvin Berlin and sung by Bing Crosby in *White Christmas:* "When you can't sleep, count your blessings instead of sheep." When you find yourself lying in bed feeling crushed under life's stresses, unable to sleep, count the blessings in your life. Run through a mental list of all the good things you can think of, and magically you will wake up the next morning feeling refreshed. Even when the world is overwhelming, there are always blessings in your life to count.

REFLECTION TIME

Self-care isn't just about getting a massage or buying yourself something shiny. It's about focusing on your mental, physical, and spiritual health. It's a lifestyle choice—and you, your family, and your business will thank you for it.

1. What is one thing you can do to reduce your stress each day?

2. Creating healthy expectations is essential. Write down three things you will work to let go of the expectation of perfection and to free up your time and your sanity.

CHAPTER 6

CONFIDENCE— YOU DA WOMAN!

We can't talk about confidence without speaking about lack of confidence, and I had never felt more inept and underqualified than during my first meeting of a governor-appointed state board.

The whole time I worried that all the older, wiser male board members would find out that I was only in my thirties and didn't have half the experience that they had. All my focus was on what I wasn't. I wasn't older, and I wasn't more experienced. At that moment, it didn't matter that by 37, I had already won a slew of business awards, as well as grown a company from $10,000 in annual sales into a multimillion-dollar international industry powerhouse. It didn't matter that I, the youngest woman on the state-level board, had been chosen to be an International Trade

Advisor on the Industry Trade Advisory Committee to the United States Congress. It didn't matter that the executive director of the Aerospace and Defense Alliance, of which I was president, recommended me to a state senator who, after interviewing me, then recommended me to the governor. Upon my appointment, I was likely the most highly recommended person on the board. None of that mattered to me at that moment. I just kept thinking that they were going to sniff me out as an imposter.

I have to give Asa Hutchinson credit. You've probably heard his name. He was the governor of Arkansas at the time, and although I had never made a political contribution to any of his campaigns and had no inside connection with him or his party, he appointed me to the state's Career Education and Workforce Development board because of my volunteer advocacy in the field of career education and workforce development, and also at the recommendation of State Senator Jane English. Of course, none of the other board members knew any of that about me. I was one of only three women on the 17-person board. I was also one of the youngest by 15 or 20 years—some of these men were literally my father's age. Sitting in tufted leather chairs (that made me feel like a little girl in her grandfather's office) at giant mahogany boardroom table surrounded by leading professionals and CEOs from all different industries, several of which were Fortune 500 companies, it was easy to be intimidated.

That feeling of personal inadequacy in business or personal or social circumstances has a name, my friends, and its name is "impostor syndrome." You can look it up if you don't believe me. Wikipedia defines imposter syndrome as "a psychological pattern in which an individual doubts their accomplishments and has a persistent internalized fear of being exposed as a fraud."

Good news: You're not crazy.

Great news: You can beat it—I did!

So, regardless all my business success and recognized community achievements, which in sum should have made it abundantly clear to me and those around me that not only did I deserve to be there, but I would be adding value and a unique, valuable perspective to the board, I was having trouble feeling that I belonged. I believed that little ole me was a great big pretender who would surely be found out and asked to leave.

But I kept reminding myself that I had every right to be there, and that the same governor who had selected and appointed me was the very same governor who had selected and appointed everyone else on the board. That self-pep talk helped me get my head on straight then, and I've gotten better since, but there are still those days when impostor syndrome still rears its ugly little head and tries to convince me I am nothing.

Feelings of inadequacy are part of the human condition—especially irrational feelings that everyone else is smarter, prettier, more qualified, etc., etc., etc. That's why it's so important to practice self-care: body, mind, and soul. If you are doing the right things to take care of your "self," you will have less trouble with feelings of inadequacy and will find new reserves and capacities abundant to share with or mentor others.

I'm often invited to speak at colleges and different business groups, and every time, even if just for a split second, I worry that I am going to disappoint the person who invited me. It's amazing how women can vacillate between pumping ourselves up and walking with our head held high and our shoulders back to doubting whether we should even be in the room. Impostor syndrome doesn't discriminate based on sex, although, more women seem to suffer from it than men.

In her research at John Brown University, Professor Eva Fast writes, "Women tend to see themselves as 'second class,' and this inhibits their emergence as a leader because it affects the group's assessment of the individual's ability to represent the group."

There is a possibility this has to do with the constant microaggressions women face in society. Having your value questioned daily in subtle ways that are almost unnoticeable will wear down your self-esteem, causing you to question the validity of your success. Just remember that you have earned your place in the room, and at the table. Your success is truly the result of your hard work. You took the opportunities and challenges you encountered and made them work for you.

Let's look at some ways to combat the impostor syndrome:

DON'T COMPARE YOURSELF TO OTHERS

One of the most unnecessary ways you damage yourself and encourage impostor syndrome is by comparing your life to someone else's social media highlight reel. It used to be that we only had to be jealous of the women who had it all together in the area where we lived. Now we get to be envious of the perfectly put-together lives of women all around the world. A great way to stop comparing yourself to others is to quit believing everything you see on social media.

It's important to remember that those photos on social media represent just a moment in time—and likely a photoshopped or filtered moment at that—that is often staged and planned in advanced. Social media followers can be bought. One of the craziest and most unrealistic things I see on social media is the desk photo. You know the one. It has coffee, flowers, macaroons, a pretty journal, etc. And for whatever reason, the "desk" always seems to be positioned on a white fur rug. That is not real life! Yet, those pictures get more likes than the real-life desk covered in contracts and papers that actually equate to dollars in the bank. Or, how about the images of models with perfect hair and makeup, wearing six-inch Louis Vuitton heels as the background for inspirational business quotes?

We all want to believe that a perfect life is possible, but the truth is that it's not. A happy life is within everyone's grasp, but a perfect life is unattainable. And trying to be perfect will make you crazy. It will make you question all of your successes, and you will never be satisfied with what you have achieved.

As I became more successful, I started to learn that the so-called perfect people were just as messed up as the rest of us. I used to flip through the society magazines and look at the women attending fancy events in their evening wear and perfect makeup. *How exciting and easy the lives of these women must be!*

Here's the inside scoop: Those events are expensive and time-consuming, and perfect hair and makeup are never perfect. Those women's hair is teased to the point of damage, and they have to wear so much makeup that they could give drag queens a run for their money. It's not cheap either. And don't get me started on the wardrobe malfunctions.

I've spent hours on hair and makeup, and hundreds of dollars, to attend multiple events in a single weekend just so I could look good in a photo that took two seconds to take. Not only do we have to bust through the glass ceiling, but if we believe social media, we must do it in between luxury vacations, facials, raising kids, and working out to get flat stomachs that make us look like supermodels. Don't forget to include plenty of time to stage photos of your laptop, morning latte, and pretty planner on a white fur rug for Instagram. The expectation of what success looks like in today's world has been drastically skewed, to say the least. The truth is that some days, success is dropping the kids off on time and making it to work with dry hair and makeup, prepared for your 9 a.m. meeting.

This isn't just a superficial problem that involves our physical appearance. Look at the way I compared my experience, or lack of, with the older men on the board. It left me feeling that I didn't belong and caused me to fall victim to the impostor syndrome. Had I gone into that first meeting grateful to be there and prepared to be productive, I wouldn't even have had the time to worry if I was an impostor. In the end, trust in yourself and your own ability.

How do you define business success? My answer is being happy and supporting yourself in what you do. If you can do that, you are successful in some way. You may be on your way up, or already there and feeling pretty happy with your level of success at the moment. Undoubtedly, you are continuing your quest for knowledge and success, or you would not have purchased this book. You have to recognize the success in your everyday life to be happy and grateful.

I always thought I'd be successful, but I didn't appreciate the journey as I should have. In all honesty, I put my nose down and worked hard, then one day someone pointed out all my success to me. That's how success happens: You work hard, enjoy the day-to-day grind, and then one day you realize that you have "made it." And that is a beautiful feeling. The day you realize that you don't have to prove yourself or try to be successful is a breath of fresh air that will leave you thinking, *Wow! This is pretty good!*

You can always spot the women who realize they have achieved success. They are kind, confident, and willing to help others. The ones who are cruel, manipulative, and self-absorbed are the ones stuck climbing or are faking it. Real success is when you can be yourself and be comfortable in your own skin where you are this day.

STOP APOLOGIZING FOR YOUR SUCCESS

How often do you say you're sorry for doing what you love and being successful at it?

I was the world's worst at explaining away material things that were a direct result of my success. When my husband bought me a new car for our 20th anniversary, I posted a blog about how hard we worked for it and how we paid cash. When someone says, "Oh, I love your Prada bag," I say, "Oh, thank you! I got it on sale, and I paid the same amount I donated to charity," when I know that no one cares how much I paid for it. Even worse, I let it sit in my closet for three years because I didn't want my material wealth to make anyone feel uncomfortable.

> Stop apologizing for your success!

During a lunch with a group of friends, I explained away an all-inclusive trip I was taking when finally, a dear friend told me in front of the group, "You make me want to smack you in the face! Stop apologizing for your success!" The rest of the women at the table chimed in and agreed.

That was an eye-opening experience for me. I always thought I was being humble. I was afraid that people wouldn't relate to me if I were successful. I dulled my shine because of the misconception that I would blind them when all I wanted was for them to feel good about themselves.

I'm not sure why I did that. Maybe I wanted people to like me. Maybe I felt guilty because I'm well aware that even though my parents divorced and I was raised by a single mom, I had more opportunities than most. Maybe it was the "it must be nice" comments on my social media post about trips I take. Maybe I felt like a fraud, and that if I enjoyed my success, someone would point out that I wasn't as successful as I thought. For whatever reason, it has been one of the biggest interpersonal battles I have had to fight.

I once even had an accountant tell me he thought I had an aversion to being wealthy, because I donated so much of my income.

The truth is, I have worked hard—very hard—to get where I am. I'm not alone. So did you! We both should be able to enjoy our success. We should be happy to fly first class, buy the shoes, make that donation, take the trip, or just live happily within our means, whatever they may be. Even if you were given more opportunity than others, remember that you did something with it! There are plenty of examples out there of people who were given everything and were never successful. You aren't one of those people.

If you worked your way up from nothing, and your friends can't encourage you to be happy in your success, get new friends. I know it seems hard, but your tribe is out there. Look inside, find out why you have guilt over your success, and let it go! Life is too short, and you've worked too hard to settle for hiding your success.

There is an old saying, "You can't pick your family, but you can pick your friends." If your family cannot or will not support you or affirm you, go make new friends. Don't worry. The family will get back in touch when they need you.

If you are concerned with what other people think of you, try this: Make a point to only be concerned what the people who pay your bills think of you. If they don't pay your bills, don't try to hide your success from them. And for you single ladies, I know plenty of men who find a successful woman extremely sexy, so don't ever worry about your success being intimidating to men! (Sometimes guys have imposter syndrome too.)

GIVE YOURSELF MORE CREDIT

Susanna, a tall young woman with long black hair that she kept in a tight side braid, had worked for me for only 90 days when it became clear that she was a true leader. Before coming to work for me, Susanna had worked for her family's small engine repair business.

Our business had grown significantly. and there were many new faces in the department where we employed her. When her department head had to be off work for two weeks because of health issues, Susanna stepped up and did the job of her manager. She led her peers and even offered solid training to those who had been there only a month less than she had. Not only was her leadership on display, so was her passion. She had an eye for quality and was well thought of by her peers. When there was a need for leadership, Susanna naturally filled that need.

At her 90-day review, we offered her a raise and told her that we wanted to make her the assistant manager of the department. Without even thinking, she said, "I don't think I'm ready. I haven't been on the job long enough, and I don't know every product in detail yet." Even though her work clearly showed that she could be a leader, she began to list all the reasons why she wasn't qualified.

Have you done something like this when success started to creep in?

In the middle of that meeting, which included other male owners and managers, I stopped her. I told her that we were going to step out of the owner-employee role for a moment and talk as two career women.

What Susanna did was something that a lot of women do. Men will say yes and then learn later, but women, they feel the need to be experts before saying yes. As a woman, you have to learn that sometimes it's necessary to jump before you are ready.

Billionaire businessman Richard Branson has been quoted as saying, "If somebody offers you an amazing opportunity, but you are not sure you can do it, say yes—then learn how to do it later!" That's how I grew my company from $10,000 a year in sales to a multimillion-dollar company. I said yes to customer requests, then figured out how to make it happen.

An old farmer turned multimillionaire aviation businessman named Joe Jett (yes, that's his real name) once told me, "Women work twice as hard to get half the respect and recognition. It's always better to bring in a female expert because she will be overly qualified on the subject."

Tom Hulseman of the Solo Cup founding family noted that out of 36 members on his District Export Council (an organization aimed at helping businesses export goods and services all over the world) only seven were women. He didn't understand why in today's world there wasn't a fifty percent membership of women. Why? The reason is that women don't step up for expert positions unless they feel overly qualified.

STEP UP YOUR GAME

The fact that corporate America largely consists of old white males is, at least partially, our fault as women in the workplace, as we have not been stepping up to contend for or claim those leadership positions. We need to be confident in our abilities. If you are not confident in your abilities, be confident in the fact that you can learn how to excel at your job, or you can learn how to create that product customers desire. Women, in general, are resourceful. We can stretch a budget to feed a family or make one dress, one pair of pants, two shirts, and two jackets look like seven days' worth of work clothes and two evening outfits. Use your intelligence and resourcefulness to learn how to do the job that you want!

This is the same reason why many women don't run for political office. A great example of a woman who stepped into her resourcefulness is Maureen Skinner. Maureen and I met at a "Women Can Run" weekend retreat that was focused on helping women prepare to run for office. A physiologist, Maureen felt like her state representative was not representing her and her beliefs. She wanted to see a change in the way her state government was run, so she decided to do it herself.

Throughout the weekend, each participant was interviewed on camera as if they were a real candidate. We would later watch the videos and evaluate ourselves. I happened to be next in line when it was time for Maureen to do her interview, and I was in awe of her confidence. When interviewed about her qualifications, she cited a government website: "'Must be 35. Must be a US citizen. Must have lived in the district for seven years.' I meet all of those requirements, plus I'm not an idiot."

While that seems simple, she was exactly right. She didn't

let the fear of not being qualified by having no experience in public office stop her from running for office. Everyone who has ever served in public office had to run before they had the experience.

I regret to say that when I was approached to run for office in my thirties, I declined because I felt like I didn't have enough knowledge of government and I wanted to be more "put together." Although I was interested in running for office, I felt I wasn't prepared. So, I made a list. Yep, a list. A list of all the things I felt that I needed to accomplish before running for office. It was a six-year plan. In six years, my younger son would be graduating high school; that way I wouldn't have to take time away from him to run. The list included things like, "Have a yoga routine I can do from anywhere," "Recover from Lasik eye surgery," and "Take a speaking class." It's embarrassing when I say it now. I thought I had to have better eyesight, no kids at home, and a daily yoga routine to be prepared to run for office.

One man, a former TV sportscaster, went on to win the position I had been asked to run for. He did a fine job, but had you laid our resumes next to each other, with my experience in business and international trade I would have appeared to be the more "qualified" candidate at the time.

BUILD YOUR CONFIDENCE

"Be scared and do it anyway."

This saying is so true. You have no idea how much faster you will reach your goals and accomplish your dreams when you just jump! Taking action and saying yes before you feel you are ready will accelerate your life and sharpen your skills.

Here are more steps you can take to build your confidence.

1. READ, WATCH, LISTEN.

Read or listen to self-help books.

I have a complete library of motivational titles on my Audible account. I also devour business books. Learning from the failures and success of business people who have achieved more than you, or who have had achievements in different areas than you, can be a constant source of inspiration.

I recommend *Outliers* by Malcolm Gladwell. That book taught me that all of the great players in the world aren't that much smarter and don't work that much harder than I do, but they take advantage of the opportunities that come their way.

A book I mentioned earlier, *Confidence Creator* by Heather Monahan, was a kick in the butt just to go out there and do it. Heather was fired from her job and decided to write a book about how she stepped out on faith to build her own company. It's both instructional and motivational when it comes to building self-confidence.

Don't just read one book a month. Read and listen constantly. If you like a book and it motivates you, put it on replay. I have a leader in my company, David, who reads the book *EntreLeadership* by Dave Ramsey at least once a year, in addition to all the other motivational and business books he reads.

Listen to motivational podcasts. Pull up a podcast on your PC and listen while you work. Goalcast.com is one I listen to daily. They have tons of content from all over the world and every different industry. As an entrepreneur, I enjoy Shrimptankpodcast.com. It features successful business people from all over the country. Hearing that others have been through the same thing as me and made it out on the other side is a significant boost of confidence that I can do it too! Plus, I really like their theme song!

Read, watch, and listen to others who motivate you.

2. GET MOTIVATED DAILY.

What do you do first thing in the morning?

If you are like millions of others in first-world countries, you start your day by scanning social media. We all know how social media can cause comparison disorder, but when used correctly, it can be a great source of motivation. I follow all kinds of motivational accounts. My days are filled with motivational quotes from leaders from every walk of life. I make a point only to follow people I find encouraging. If I start comparing myself, I unfollow until I am in a better place personally.

I also read a chapter from the book of Proverbs in the Bible daily. Proverbs has 31 chapters, which works out that I read the entire book every month. Solomon was the wisest ruler who ever lived. That gives me wisdom and motivation to face any challenges the day brings.

One small but impactful change that helps me start the day on a positive note was that I stopped watching the news first thing in the morning. Hearing about all the negative things going on in the world first thing in the morning put me in a negative mood. So, I changed my routine and started listening to uplifting music every morning instead.

3. CREATE A VISION BOARD.

I thought this was super cheesy for years. I admit it. As I gained success, I thought I had moved past needing a visual reminder of what I wanted out of life. But the truth is, having a visual reminder of what you're fighting for gives you the confidence to achieve your dreams and goals.

Early in my marriage and career, I had magazine cutouts of cars and homes we wanted, as well as a list of accomplishments we hoped to achieve. I taped that list to the refrigerator in our 900-square-foot home in base housing provided by the Air Force in Jacksonville, Arkansas.

That daily reminder helped keep me going as I worked three jobs and was a full-time college student. Today, the visual reminders, such as a yacht and a million-dollar check to local charities, remind me to have confidence when I walk into contract negations. I know

> Keeping a constant eye on your life goals gives you the confidence to walk into any situation with the power to change your life.

that not achieving my goals is scarier than the executives who sit across the board room table from me. I am working toward achieving something bigger than anything that I face daily.

Keeping a constant eye on your life goals gives you the confidence to walk into any situation with the power to change your life. I no longer keep the vision board on my fridge. It's evolved to the point where it's now a poster board hanging on the wall in my closet. Every morning when I get ready, I am forced to look at my goals and dreams as I prepare for my day. It keeps me focused on what I truly want in life.

4. TAKE AN INVENTORY.

Take an inventory of where you are in life and pay specific attention to the ways you are awesome. List your accomplishments. While it is vital to self-reflect in order to grow into a better version of yourself, don't forget what you have overcome to get where you are. You weren't born breaking glass ceilings and throat-punching stereotypes; you had to work to get here. Even if you are just starting out in your career, you had to decide to go for the life you wanted. You took steps to get the degree, apply for the job, conquer the interview, and even start the business.

* * *

I once got the "OMG, what am I doing here?" nerves just before walking into a conference where I was speaking on a panel filled with executives who were old enough to be my grandfather. They were running Fortune 500 companies while my company had not even reached five million in sales yet.

So I went into the bathroom, locked myself in a stall, and assumed the Wonder Woman position. (Yes, it's a thing.) As I stood there with my hands on my hips, legs in a sturdy stance, head held high, this is what I said:

I started a company with no experience that now sells millions. I earned a college degree while working three jobs, adopting a son, being pregnant and on bedrest all while maintaining a hot marriage. I negotiated deals with the largest aircraft manufacturers in the world. I was in foreclosure, and almost lost my house, but it didn't kill me, I can handle this! I deserve to be here, and I deserve to be heard.

I always make sure to remind myself that even the worst-case scenario won't kill me. Even if no one likes what I have to say, they aren't going to stone me to death or take my children away. And if I'm not going to die or lose my family, then nothing that happens to me is really that scary.

I walked out of that bathroom stall, went into the conference room, and killed it! Every single one of the speakers complimented me when it was over. On top of that, two of them asked me to serve on boards with them shortly thereafter.

There are some days when you wake up so confident and positive that nothing can stop you. Then there are the days when you find yourself standing in the Wonder Woman pose, locked in a bathroom stall, giving yourself a reminder of how awesome you are.

If you are stepping into a situation that makes you question yourself, refer to your list of what you have already accomplished before walking in. Whenever you find yourself questioning your confidence, don't forget about your tribe. Reach out to those people who will encourage you and cheer you on when you win and straighten your crown when you lose. That's why I'm on a group text with several of my tribe members, and I have more than once sent out an SOS for some encouragement and prayers when my confidence was low. I cannot emphasize enough the importance of a text from a true friend who told me, "You are a Rockstar!" at just the right moment.

GET YOUR MONEY RIGHT

A huge step in building confidence is to get your money right. You've heard the term "financial freedom" tossed around, but have you ever thought about what financial freedom could mean to your confidence level?

Financial freedom is literally having enough money to provide the ability to do what's best for you—*the ability to do what you want, when you want, and how you want.*

If you have financial freedom, you can walk away from a job that doesn't excite you. Financial freedom allows you the freedom to have the choice to walk away from a bad boss or a company culture that is toxic or demeaning.

If you're working to make ends meet, you will be forced to stay in a position where you're not happy. If you're working to pay your mortgage every month, you won't have the confidence to step away from a toxic environment to seek better employment or start your own business.

You may be thinking, *Well, that's easy for you to say. You have a successful company that allows you to be financially free.*

Yes, I make good money, and I have a comfortable lifestyle, but it was the actions I took before my company was successful that gave me the freedom to take risks. And I still take those same actions now that my income has grown so I can continue to have the financial freedom to be confident in my ability to decide my path.

STEP #1: LIVE WITHIN YOUR MEANS.

What does that mean?

It means that if you don't have the money to give 10 percent of your salary to charity, save 20 percent for an emergency, and use the rest to pay down debt and cover all your bills, you're living outside of your means.

Don't worry, you are not alone when it comes to living outside of what you can afford. Have you ever watched the TV series *American Greed*? It tells the stories of people doing anything to keep up the appearance of wealth. There are countless cautionary tales about millionaires losing everything. You know the script. People live lavish lifestyles, fly on private jets, drive $100,000 cars, and sail the world on yachts, then suddenly declare bankruptcy. It doesn't matter if you make $20,000 a year or $20,000,00 a year—if you are spending everything you have, you are not financially free. You end up in a cycle of extending yourself to pay for a lifestyle that is beyond your means. And you're literally a slave to your debt-financed lifestyle, no better really than a slave, as you must must work every day to keep the roof over your head.

The steps to achieving financial freedom are the same on a salary of $20,000 or $2,000,000. My son made roughly $20,000 a year when he was 20 and had the freedom to switch jobs when he wanted, or even take a few weeks of unpaid time off if he desired. And no, I didn't support him. He paid for his own apartment, car, insurance, etc. He chose not to live beyond his means, and he saved.

He knew that his cost of living was roughly $1,000 a month. So every Friday when he got paid, he had an auto transfer of $250 into his "bill account." That ensured that he would always have the money to pay his bills for the following month and wouldn't spend his money on nonessentials. He used the rest of his money to live on. At 20 years old, he always had a month's worth of living expenses in the bank at a minimum. He never had to worry if he would have money for his car payment or rent. If he wants a nicer car or home, he will put an increased amount in his bill account to ensure that he can still live on the rest, plus he has a down payment if needed.

Having money set aside in an account that you can only access by getting in the car and going to the bank to pay your bills allows you to have one less thing to think about. It also gives you the confidence of knowing that you have the option to step away from toxic work and living environments. I personally believe that is the first step in financial freedom.

The next step is looking at the actual money you have left to live on. This keeps you aware of your goals of becoming financially free. You are less likely to go out to dinner or buy that bag when your actual financial situation is at the front of your mind.

That's why I live on what is referred to as a zero-dollar budget. I have every dollar allocated. First, I tithe 10 percent of my income. Then, I set my money for bills aside. Then, I put money into IRAs and a cash savings account. I cannot explain the feeling of confidence knowing that I have a year's worth of mortgage payments set aside. Then, all the money I have left is for living: gas, food, fun, etc.

STEP #2: CONSIDER A FINANCIAL ADVISOR.

You don't have to be rich or already have a savings plan in place to benefit from a financial advisor. Choose one who teaches financial literacy. The right financial advisor can help lay out a plan for debt reduction and savings.

Many people use programs or ideas such as Crown Financial Principles, or the method that Dave Ramsey teaches in his books and websites to get started. Crown.org has a ton of great resources for budgeting. My favorite are different calculators that show how much you need to save for retirement, how to snowball your way out of debt, and how much money and time you will save by adding a little extra to your monthly mortgage. Primerica has a website that offers a financial needs assessment to give you a complete idea of what your finances look like and what they should look like to reach your goals.

Even if you choose to begin your journey without a financial advisor, I suggest joining up with a group of people who are working toward the same goal of financial freedom. Just like having a workout partner increases your chances of being successful in achieving a healthy lifestyle, having a partner or support group in the journey to financial freedom increases your chance of success. Plus, having a group that you can visit with when you bring your lunch to work makes it more fun when choosing financial freedom over eating lunch out.

STEP #3: JOIN A SALES GROUP.

I attribute a large portion of my success and confidence to skills I learned while in a multilevel marketing company (MLM). I learned to sell. I learned business basics. I had a network of extremely successful people around me. I had access to motivational books and speakers that would have cost me a fortune had I not been involved in the MLM company. The products I sold were excellent, and just like everything else, it was hard work, but it was the conferences they hosted that really changed my life.

MLM companies spend millions on bringing in the best speakers and motivators in the world for their conferences. The MLM company Quixtar—you probably first heard of it as Amway—was my first business school, and the lessons I learned from my experience in MLM would shape how I did business for the rest of my life. If you're interested in making some extra money, I highly suggest looking into MLM companies—it's an excellent way of earning extra money and building your personal confidence.

Another example: I saw a woman who was quiet and

meek as a church mouse start selling Rodan Fields skincare and turn into a confident force to be reckoned with. She not only made it to a top selling position and received a new car, but it changed her whole life. She now speaks with confidence, walks with her head held high, and teaches other women to do the same.

STEP #4: ENJOY THE CONFIDENCE THAT COMES WITH FINANCIAL FREEDOM.

If you are lucky enough to have very little debt, you are already a step ahead. If you can relieve yourself of the stress that comes with worrying about money, I promise you will get a much more significant boost in your confidence than you will from any bag you can't afford.

Whether you start by saving or paying off debt, all methods begin by deciding what you want more: the perception of a certain lifestyle or the confidence that comes with financial freedom. Really ask yourself the tough questions:

- Why do I have debt?

- Why don't I have savings?

- Why do I purchase things I can't afford?

- What feeling do I get from that expensive bag or those dinners out with friends?

- Is it a temporary rush of confidence?

- Do I love how I look in new clothes?

- Do I love going out with friends?

- Does that feeling last when I look at my bank account or go to the job I hate?

Then comes the most important question of all: *Are you committed to getting to a better place with your finances?*

It's not easy. Planning for financial freedom is like starting a new healthy lifestyle. The foods we eat make us feel good for a moment, but that feeling only lasts a short period. The price of overeating and not exercising is having clothes that don't fit, losing your breath as you walk up the stairs, and just overall dissatisfaction with your appearance. Doesn't that make you want to make a change?

Change isn't easy. It's no fun to give up our favorite junk food and go sweat it out at the gym, but once you notice that your clothes are looser and you hear people comment on the weight you've lost, it becomes worth it. And that feeling lasts much longer than the taste of good food.

It's the same with finances. Saying no to eating lunch with girlfriends is not fun. Not buying that new belt or pair of shoes seems cruel at first, but paying off that credit card bill is an amazing feeling! What's more, watching your savings account grow is better than any temporary feelings of shopping bliss.

If you trust the process, you will get to the point where you have the confidence to walk into a toxic situation and say, "We are going to have to make this better, or I am going elsewhere." Whether it's a toxic work environment or a toxic relationship, being financially free opens up a whole world of options.

In her book *Confidence Creator,* Heather Monahan

states that after she was fired, she had saved enough money to take time off to write her book. Because she had her money right, she had the opportunity to change her life and the lives of thousands who read her book.

What dreams are your finances stopping you from achieving? How has your confidence suffered because of financial worries and concerns? Do you find yourself working under demeaning superiors because you are afraid to lose your job? Are you afraid to lose your job because it's the only source of income you have and the only way to pay your bills?

It's time to make a change in your financial world. It's time to start putting money in the bank and confidence in your life.

ELIMINATE THE WORD *UM*

Some of the best speaking advice I ever received was about how to stop saying the word *um*.

Um is a non-word filler while you gather your next thought. You have to remove *um* and replace it with silence. The tricky part is learning how to become comfortable in that silence. It's uncomfortable at first, but once you've done it a few times, it becomes natural.

Whether you're trying to remove phrases that ask for validation from your vocabulary, or if you're making a conscious effort to stop saying um, there is no better way to help you break the habit (while quelling any fear of the silence being awkward) than to watch a video of yourself giving a speech. It will provide you with a whole new perspective, and video proof, that using more active language while including brief silences is not nearly as uncomfortable or awkward as you're making it out to be. If anything, the opposite is true, and you will sound more confident and assertive. Think of it as taking a dramatic pause to heighten the emphasis of your statement. And as an added bonus, the silence gives the listener a chance to process what you have just said, making your words more impactful.

It seems odd to talk about silence in a chapter about speaking with confidence. When you replace words like "um" or "like" with silence, you're taking control of your mind. I know this sounds hokey, but this practice will help you succeed in many ways. Not only will you begin to speak with more confidence, but you will also be able to keep your emotions in check while reducing stress and anxiety.

When someone puts you on the spot and asks a question you may not be ready for, stay silent for a second. Collect your thoughts, then answer with confidence. They say silence is golden, but a few seconds of silence can be a nice confidence booster as well! It all starts with making a conscious effort to practice this in your daily lives.

DON'T BE AFRAID OF FAILURE

Failure is simply a stepping-stone to success. Failure is not final. Failing is actually good for your confidence—provided you get back up and try again. The more you fail, the more you learn. It depends how you view "failing."

Thomas A. Edison, inventor of the incandescent lightbulb, is quoted as saying, after thousands of failures to invent the lightbulb, "I have not failed. I've just found 10,000 ways that it won't work." Hey, look above you. You're probably reading this under a lightbulb, and had he quit, we'd all be carrying pockets full of candles.

Once you try and fail, you realize that failure won't kill you, and in fact "failure" actually teaches you more than success does.

Learning that failure didn't kill me was a huge catalyst for my success. I have had many small failures in my life, but surviving an enormous failure that I thought would crush me gave me the confidence to try anything.

It started when I went after a new product line that my company had no experience with. I was working 70-hour weeks at the time. My husband worked a full-time job, then would come design product in the evenings while our sons played in my office. We had family "picnics" at our conference table for our nightly dinners.

I had invested every penny into that new product line, so we were functionally broke. I almost had to close my business. My home was in foreclosure, and my family life was stressful because there was no life. There was only work. We were so poor that I was feeding my kids peanut butter sandwiches. Not peanut butter and jelly sandwiches, just peanut butter.

Eventually, I failed at the product line and had to scrap it. I failed at being a mother to my sons. I failed at being a wife to my husband. The shame and exhaustion of failure nearly broke me. It nearly broke my family. I wanted to quit.

But I didn't quit. I survived.

I survived a failure so big and public that everyone was

lined up to say, "I told you so." I'd been advised, "Stick to what you know," and told not to waste my time on a chance. And I didn't listen. I survived to prevail.

I survived a failure that almost cost me my mental health and my marriage.

But I'm still here! I'm still standing, and I'm more successful than before. My kids are good, and my marriage is stronger than ever! Looking back on that time in my life now, I realize that if that failure didn't kill me, I can try anything.

Failure is just evidence that you are willing to succeed.

REFLECTION TIME

What failure have you survived that you thought would kill you?

What did you learn from that failure?

What are you not doing now because you're afraid to fail?

WE'RE ALL IN THIS TOGETHER

Dear Reader,

Are you ready to be who you know you can be?

I don't think that it's any surprise that most ambitious women want to be both feminine and fierce. Social media is littered with photos of gorgeous women in high heels with sayings like, "I'm not trying to find a rich husband, I'm trying to be a rich wife." And, "Be the CEO your parents wanted you to marry." It's widely accepted by those under 40 that a woman can be both beautiful and the boss.

We all have that one friend or relative who is the epitome of the 1960s angry feminist. Mine is a beloved relative. She is a no-bra-wearing, non-leg-shaving, man-hating (except for two) feminist. She can hold her own door, and pee standing up! No kidding (she proved it once thanks to a handy funnel tool). At the beginning of my marriage, she called my husband an idiot daily and educated him on every male inadequacy. And of course, I heard comments from her anytime I fixed my husband a plate of food or wore an outfit because he liked it.

I am all about female empowerment, and I firmly believe we need all types of people on each end of the spectrum fighting for the cause of equality. We need women marching in the streets, casting votes in Congress, and negotiating in the boardroom. However, I am proudly a feminine feminist—not just in my attire, but in my attitude as well.

My younger son once made the joke: "You want equal pay, yet you expect me to hold the door for you?" Well, in a word, yes! While I do, without a doubt, expect my sons to hold the door for ladies, I can hold my own, and be grateful to the gentleman that chooses to hold it for me.

Once, when I stepped off a transport bus at a manufacturing event, a gentleman offered me his hand in getting off the bus. I gladly accepted it and thanked him. He then offered the women directly behind me his hand, but she said, "I've got this." Then, referring to me, she said, "She must be somebody's wife." In one sentence, she was rude to someone offering her help, and fed into the stereotype that a feminine woman can't work in my industry. As a woman in manufacturing, I have to fight against that stereotype daily, and in that case at the event, it was being vocalized by a woman in my own field.

Way to win one for feminism, lady!

Do you think that woman's attitude toward the gentleman and myself will turn that man into an ally for women in his industry? How does putting another woman down help promote equality? It doesn't. It promotes the idea that women are catty and that feminists are man-hating assholes.

* * *

I was raised by a single mom who taught me to breathe fire. She was one of a rare few women in her professional field. She coached my softball team, hung with the big boys as a sharpshooter, and taught me to watch what men do, so I could learn from them. Yet, she was never a man-hater.

She never put a man down for trying to help her. Maybe it was because she had three younger brothers whom she kept up with and respected at the same time. While my mother was in law school, I spent most of my time with my grandmother, my nana.

Nana was a true Southern belle. She was the first feminine feminist I ever knew. A woman before her time, she woke up before her husband to put on her makeup. But after 12 years of marriage, she caught her husband cheating and divorced him. (This was in the late 1950s, mind you, and women didn't file for divorces back then.) My grandmother fought successfully to keep her home, received no child support, and went from being high society to working in a Piggly Wiggly to support her children. She had gone from being a married stay-at-home socialite in the 1950s who wore furs and attended events around town to being a meatpacker.

Nana later married her ally, my papa, having managed to pay off her home before they wed. Even though Papa told her she didn't have to work, she still did. They traveled the world and sailed on a yacht on the weekend. Then she packed meat during the week until she retired when I was about five years old.

My nana taught me to fix my husband's plate of food first, and that Papa (or the man of the house) always got the big piece of chicken. She told me not to disrespect my husband in public, and not to allow him to disrespect me either. I don't ever remember my grandfather disrespecting her in public, but I do remember a rather fierce argument at their home.

One night, Nana called Papa by his full name like he was a disobedient third grader in trouble at school. "I will not stand for that s---!" she had lectured. "You will not speak to me that way!"

I distinctly remember Papa's response. "Aww, hell, woman" (which in that house meant, *yes, ma'am*). That fight was over.

Nana told us how she decided that it wasn't right for the men at the country club to have a men's-only cigar room. She recalls, "We stood up on our hind legs and told them we were coming in!" And that's how the Hot Springs Country Club got its first co-ed cigar room. She stood her ground. She fought for equality in her world.

Even with her perfect hair and makeup, she would climb on a roof to patch a hole or hop on a giant sailboat and captain that thing right along with my grandfather. And she worked. She worked hard. She even wore pants to church in the 1980s, but she never lost her Southern grace and charm!

* * *

Women come in all shapes, sizes, colors, and levels of femininity. And we need all types to join together and fight for equality. We need to embrace each other's differences and place value on those differences. Guess what? The bleach blonde in the tight dress who uses her curves to make sales also needs your respect and support just as much as a Supreme Court Justice. The blonde is not killing our cause. She's working with what she's got. Our job is not to put her down, but to become an ally and join together in the fight for being recognized for our skills, not our sex. You can't lift women up by tearing them down.

You can be a high-, medium-, or low-maintenance feminist as long as you are committed to maintaining yourself. And there is nothing wrong with having a man (if you so choose) support you emotionally or financially. The important thing is that you have a man who is an ally, a partner, or even a male feminist, who believes you can and should have every right to work your way to the top.

Some don't understand where I'm coming from when I say *equality*. To me, equality means that a woman makes equal pay for equal work, has equal access to capital financing for business, and has the right to have her tubes tied anytime she wants, just like a man can go have a vasectomy anytime he wants. (At the printing of this book, medical doctors in private hospitals can require a woman to be at least 25 years of age, have had at least one child, and be married before they will tie her tubes. A man only needs a check for $499 to have a vasectomy.)

So, if a woman chooses to be a stay-at-home mom, that is her choice, and it should be respected. If a woman chooses never to marry, that is her choice. If a woman chooses to have a career, children, and be a submissive wife, that is her choice, and it should be respected.

Remember, if we lift as we rise, then we will all rise together.

ABOUT THE AUTHOR

Gina Radke is a successful business owner, entrepreneur, speaker, investor and economic influencer. Owner and CEO of an Aerospace Manufacturing company, Galley Support Innovations, Gina uses her international business experience to serve as an Industry Trade Advisor to the US Congress, mentor start up companies, help companies scale and teach young people about finances. Gina has mentored entrepreneurs from across the globe and is well known for her involvement in community service, and empowering others with economic opportunities.

Gina married her husband, Wade in 1998 on the Little Rock Airforce Base where Wade served as an Airman in the US Air Force. Gina and Wade have three legal sons, but many others who have called them mom and dad. Huge advocates for adoption and foster care, the Radke's have volunteered as mentors and board members with Immerse Arkansas. Immerse is a housing and community program for children who have aged out of the foster care system.

Gina is a proud member of Rotary International's Club 99. She is active in both state and local chambers where she advocates for business and education matters.

Gina has used wit and grace to navigate her way to the top of the boy's club.

www.ginaradke.com

Reach out to the author on the
following Social Media Outlets:
Twitter: @ginaradke
Instagram: @ginaradke
Linkedin: Gina Radke
Facebook: Gina Radke

Requests for speaking engagements may be
made via email to info@ginaradke.com